109,95,84

P9-APA-342

CULTS IN AMERICA

CULTS
in America

Programmed for Paradise

WILLA APPEL

Holt, Rinehart and Winston / New York

Copyright © 1983 by Willa Appel

All rights reserved, including the right to reproduce
this book or portions thereof in any form.

Published by Holt, Rinehart and Winston,
383 Madison Avenue, New York, New York 10017.

Published simultaneously in Canada by Holt, Rinehart
and Winston of Canada, Limited.

Library of Congress Cataloging in Publication Data
Appel, Willa.
Cults in America.
Includes bibliographical references.
1. Cults—United States.   2. United States—Religion—
1960-   I. Title.
BL2530.U6A66   1983   291'.0973   82-15538
ISBN: 0-03-054836-5
First Edition

Designer: Victoria Gomez
Printed in the United States of America
10 9 8 7 6 5 4 3 2 1

ISBN 0-03-054836-5

291.0973
Ap485c

For my father and mother

244015

274012

Acknowledgments

Many people assisted me during the writing of this book. I would especially like to thank Elizabeth Janeway, whose ideas and suggestions stimulated my own thinking and whose generosity and encouragement were invaluable. I could not have written the book without all the people who so unstintingly gave their time to speak with me about their experiences in cults; I thank them. Michael Brooks's support during the initial stages and Carla Levine's during the latter were very helpful. I am grateful for the encouragement and excellent advice of my editor, Natalie Chapman. I thank too my dear friend Maureen Liebl, who listened, read, and offered thoughtful comments and, equally important, enthusiasm. Finally, I thank Allan Talbot, who not only read and advised me on draft upon draft of the manuscript, but who also managed to retain a balanced perspective and sense of humor throughout.

Contents

CULTS IN AMERICA

1 ≡

THE CULT PHENOMENON

In the past two decades there has been a proliferation of cults in America. They have appeared in a variety of forms—as Eastern religions, self-help groups, and Christian revival movements—and they have attracted unprecedented numbers of followers. Many of these groups were spin-offs from the counterculture movement of the 1960s, whose repudiation of society resulted in widespread social experimentation. In a matter of years, however, most of the sixties-style egalitarian communes had folded, giving way to another type of utopian group, the cult.

Few people appeared to take cults very seriously until November 1978, when nine hundred Americans died in Jonestown, Guyana. That tragedy focused press attention on the existence in the United States of many other groups like the People's Temple, similarly organized around a messianic leader, similarly isolated from the rest of the world, and with similarly fervent beliefs. Suddenly cults boomeranged into the national consciousness.

In fact, cults had been a subject of controversy before Jonestown. Parents alarmed at the effect of these groups on their children sought some means of redress. Their furor had even provoked a few governmental investigations. Yet most hearings on cults produced more questions than answers. Frustrated parents turned to "deprogrammers," the professional vigilantes who, in true cloak-and-dagger style, "snatched" cult members and forcibly detained and deconverted them. The legality of their actions generated still more doubts.

Indeed, the cult phenomenon raises fundamental questions about the nature of our society. Such fundamental questions as the intent of the law and the boundaries of personal and legal jurisdiction are challenged. How far can religious practices go before they infringe on the other freedoms guaranteed by the Constitution? What is the difference between the advocacy of religious belief and brainwashing, and how can this distinction be established?

These questions remain. The controversy over cults, however, has increased to the degree that it is almost impossible to assess the phenomenon with any dispassion. Even the term *cult* is loaded. A battle-camp mentality has made objective discussion impossible. On the one side are the parents, mental-health professionals, journalists, and lawyers who feel that cults represent a new and untoward danger both to the individuals involved and to society as a whole. On the other are the cults themselves. Armed with money, political influence, and the First Amendment, they have attacked those who dare criticize them, retaining a battery of lawyers to discourage any further criticism. There is an ironic twist to this conflict. The anticultists who advocate legal measures to curtail the cults appear to be political reactionaries, while the cults, many of which are oriented toward the political right, have become a bulwark for the First Amendment.

While not immune to the controversy surrounding cults, I will nevertheless try to make some sense of the phenomenon. What are cults? Why do they arise in the first place? Who is likely to join a cult, and why? Who leads one? What goes on in a cult, and what happens to an individual as a result of cult membership? What dangers do they pose? This book addresses these questions.

Cults are not a new phenomenon in America. Our history has been punctuated by periods of cult efflorescence. In New York State in the early 1800s, for instance:

> Prophets and preachers of every description began to swarm across the countryside, and eventually Palmyra itself became the geographical center of much evangelical activity, a place where innumerable residents believed literally in hell fire, original sin and redemption through baptism, in the laying on of hands and speaking in tongues, and in the approaching Millennium, an era of a thousand years when Jesus Christ would return to earth and reign in peace and glory.
>
> Some frontier religions were mildly eccentric, while the others were extremely bizarre. Possibly the most flamboyant messiah of all was Isaac Bullard. Clad in nothing but a bearskin loincloth, he led his troop of adherents from Vermont through New York and Ohio and finally south to Missouri, proclaiming a religion compounded of free love, communism and dirt—Bullard often boasting that he hadn't washed in seven years.[1]

In many ways, cults have remained remarkably unchanged over the centuries. Their form, content, even the controversy they generate have been surprisingly consistent. Cults are groups of people who share a common vision and who see themselves as separate from the rest of the world—some withdrawing literally from society, others merely withdrawing psychologically. The internal structure of cults varies; they may be ill-defined, loosely related groups of equals who share responsibilities and power, or they may be rigidly hierarchical. A cult may also be described as an evolutionary phase in the development of a religion or a political entity, an early stage in the growth of an institution, though in fact many cults do not survive to reach maturity.

What a cult is helps to explain why it provokes controversy. By their very nature, cults alienate ordinary citizens, for they defy the existing social order. Seeing themselves as separate from the rest of the world, with a separate ideology and a different life-style, cult members stand in opposition to society, denying, in greater or lesser degree, its legitimacy. Believing themselves to be different from and superior to the rest of the world, cult members tend to ignore the rules that govern less exalted citizens. At odds with society in the first place, this antagonism can easily lead to confrontation. In reaction, it is not surprising to find that the established order will strike back. But the degree to which it does depends upon how threatening the cults are.

Most of the so-called cults that presently abound in this country can be characterized as millenarian. The term *millenarism* derives from the prophesied millennium, the thousand-year reign of Christ. Movements that embody this vision express a longing and a belief in a salvation that will take place here on earth. Though millenarian movements have existed throughout recorded history and in virtually every society, each particular version reflects the culture in which it arises. All, however, share certain fundamental characteristics: they assume there is a grand plan to history and that present events are building to a preordained catastrophe. In this scenario, there are only two available roles—those of saint and sinner. The millennium occurs as a direct result of the struggle between these warring camps.

Most millenarian movements are also messianic; that is, salvation is orchestrated by a human emissary of God, and it depends upon total commitment to that messiah.

Much of the activity in millenarian groups has to do with preparing for Judgment Day. Ecstatic behavior—trance, possession, hysteria, and paranoia—commonly figure. Followers also tend to disregard secular laws and morals, which, in the atmosphere of impending revolution, appear inconsequential. As a result, aberrant behavior, including the unconstrained expression of aggression, is a recurring feature.

The early history of the Mormon church illustrates the aggression that typifies many millenarian movements. Although Mormons claimed, with some reason, that they were being persecuted by the "Gentiles," the causes of the conflict derived in large part from their own attitudes. Believing themselves to be morally superior to the remainder of humanity and thus not bound by ordinary laws, and anticipating an imminent Judgment Day that would result in the subjugation of all non-Mormons by the Latter-Day Saints, the Mormons were predisposed to violent confrontation with their neighbors. One church leader, Sampson Avard, actually sanctioned robbing and pillaging: "Know ye not, brethren," he preached, "that it will soon be your privilege to go out on a scout on the borders of the new settlements, and to take to yourselves . . . the goods of the ungodly Gentiles? For it is written, the riches of the Gentiles shall be consecrated to my people, the house of Israel. And thus you will waste away the Gentiles by robbing and plundering them of their property; and in this way we will build up the Kingdom of God. . . ." [2]

Aggression in millenarian movements is not necessarily directed outward. In Melanesia in the late nineteenth century, a whole genre of millenarian cults called "Cargo Cults" evolved in the wake of European colonization. The indigenous population resented the intrusion of the colonizers yet, at the same time, were intrigued by the material goods, the "cargo," they introduced. Their cults embodied this ambivalence. They predicted an imminent millennium that would arrive in the form of an enormous flood, washing the white man off the face of Melanesia while leaving his goods intact. In anticipation, natives destroyed their own villages, burned their homes and crops, and retired to the hills to wait.

The timing of the millennium varies in different millenarian groups. Members of Cargo Cults believed it to be imminent. Other groups do not foresee Judgment Day in the near future; while some, like the Jehovah's Witnesses, predict its arrival and then routinely postpone the date when it fails to materialize on schedule.

Attitudes toward the past also vary: many glorify the past, prophesying a return to an idealized image of the "good old days." The Ghost Dance of 1889, for example, took place at a time when the survival of the Plains Indians was imperiled. White settlers had taken over the land and decimated the buffalo, thereby jeopardizing the survival of the Indians. The Ghost Dance was propagated by the prophet Wovoka, a Paiute Indian also known as Jack Wilson. He predicted the day when the world of the white man and all the changes he had brought would be destroyed. He urged the Indians to dance to hasten the millennium. Because paradise featured the return of long-dead ancestors and herds of near-extinct buffalo, the cult was called the Ghost Dance. According to Wovoka's vision, old ways would be resumed and all the tribes would live peacefully together, though they had never done so in the past. Only those Indians who had adopted white ways were to be excluded from paradise. Anthropologists have classified this type of millenarian activity, which glorifies the past, as a revitalization movement.

The most dramatic revitalization movement of recent years is Ayatollah Khomeini's conservative Moslem crusade. In a reaction against the modernization that the mullahs believe has corrupted the purity of Islam, Khomeini has outlawed as "satanic" all those elements that symbolize this corruption in Iran: Western dress, music, and education. Like the Ghost Dance, the Iranian revitalization movement condemns all those who have embraced these "modern" ways.

All millenarian movements are critical of the present, because all arise from opposition to the reigning social order. Yet as these examples demonstrate, the form this opposition takes is not always the same: some, like the Cargo Cults, totally withdraw from the world, with members destroying their material possessions and means of livelihood. Others, like those of Ayatollah Khomeini and Wovoka, glorify the past. Still other groups advocate a physical move from one geographical location to another: Marcus Garvey's Back to Africa movement of the 1920s tried to "repatriate" black Americans to Africa. Garvey, a visionary from Jamaica, came to the United States in 1916 to found a mass movement dedicated to racial redemption. Nationhood, he believed, was the key to salvation. A more recent visionary who believed wholesale migration was the answer was Jim Jones. He moved his group from place to place, finally settling them in Guyana to establish a new and pure society.

Attitudes within millenarian movements often change over time. A typical pattern is for active rebellion to be followed by passive withdrawal. The failure of activism often results in a turning inward. The ideologically aggressive Ghost Dance was supplanted by the Peyote Cult after the massacre at Wounded Knee devastated the morale of the surviving Indians. The Peyote Cult represented a total withdrawal into a passive, drug-induced spiritual world. Similarly, following Garvey's arrest and deportation to Jamaica in 1927, many of his followers transferred their allegiance to Father Divine, whose approach to racism was simply to deny its existence.

Some people have assumed that millenarian movements are movements of the oppressed. That is not strictly true. They usually occur in groups whose expectations have undergone sudden change, not among the chronically desperate, who are often resigned to their fate. Millenarian activity is a classic response when people feel frustrated and confused, when they face changes that violate cherished expectations. Disaster, economic depressions, wars, droughts, and plagues often precipitate a millenarian response.

The failure of new aspirations can also be a catalyst. Marcus Garvey's post–World War I crusade is an example of this type of millenarism. During the war years, 875,000 blacks fled the South, enticed by promises of steady work, better education, and a just society. Conditions in the fabled North, however, were not what they had been led to expect by northern industrial recruiters. Industry hired blacks only when orders piled up, and labor unions persistently refused blacks membership. The most humiliating rejection occurred when blacks tried to enlist in the armed forces during World War I and were turned down. Yet the new oppression was not a simple replacement of the old. Jobless, crowded into alien tenement ghettos, and despised, they had nevertheless left the old feudal order of the South. Their ideas about what they had a right to expect had changed radically. The immediate aftermath of the war and the great migration was an explosion of racial violence. Over three dozen race riots erupted during the war years and the Ku Klux Klan experienced a revival. Competition for jobs, especially during the Depression following the war, was a crucial ingredient. As important, however, was the changed attitudes of many blacks. They were no longer willing or able to turn the other cheek. The old order had changed irrevocably. Garvey appealed to those who had migrated north only to discover many of the same inequalities. He aggressively championed black rights and black self-determination. And he was the first to support and organize black-owned businesses. It was only after repeated disappointments that he abandoned the hope of achieving true equality and selfhood for blacks in America and advocated return to the African "homeland."

In the broadest terms, millenarian movements develop in periods of social breakdown and transition. Rapid social change disrupts traditional beliefs and values as well as the ability of a social system to meet the expectations of its members. The result is disorientation and alienation, for values do not just exist "out there" but are internalized as part of an individual's identity. Contact with different social groups, whether through colonization, wars, or modernization, for example, often triggers a millenarian response. These movements represent both a reaction to frustration and the attempt to re-create reality, to reestablish a personal identity in situations where the old world view has lost meaning.

Change, however, does not affect all groups equally within a society. Some are better able to adjust than others. Generally, millenarism appeals to those who have no political voice, who lack effective organization, and who do not have at their disposal regular, institutionalized means of redress. People who are firmly rooted in society—in kinship, community, and political groups—are less likely to become involved in millenarian alternatives. Marginality, in short, is a key factor in millenarian appeal.

Despite the apparent novelty and recent proliferation of cults, there is no evidence to suggest that they represent anything radically new. In size, origin, and evolution, the present cults tend to conform generally to those of the past. Though the form and function of cults transcend cultural and historical boundaries, the specific characteristics of cults do vary, reflecting the particular culture in which they develop. Cult members today, for example, are not from the traditionally disaffected classes. The overwhelming majority are young, white, and middle-class. Why these, the privileged members of American society, should be abandoning the mainstream is perplexing.

In part, the current wave of cults is an outgrowth of and a reaction to the activism of the 1960s. Many of those who perceived that they had failed to reform the social system or to end the Vietnam war eventually turned to a more passive spiritualism. In the course of a decade, the antiwar movement underwent a transformation from the politics of protest to open revolt and finally to total withdrawal, as a perceived impotence to fundamentally change society gave way to a repudiation of activism itself.

Though turning inward was not the exclusive response of young people, the young were at the forefront of a nationwide reaction, and they tended most often to opt for the more extreme millenarian alternatives. Society was rejected wholesale; a new world was envisioned to replace it. The Weathermen represented one type of millenarian response to the frustrations of social activism. Utopian communes were another version of the same response. They too condemned conventional values, but rather than break shop windows or burn draft cards, their members retreated to isolated areas to live like an earlier generation of pioneers. Both types of millenarism shared a powerful sense of community apart and at odds with the dominant society. Both defied "establishment" values, flaunting political and sexual liberation.

The Vietnam war challenged cherished beliefs about the basic goodness of America and democratic ideas. That challenge, however, extended beyond the war. Social institutions and values had been changing since World War II. Sexual mores, the structure of the family, and the role of the schools and churches in the socialization of the young had all been in a prolonged process of transformation. Cults were yet another response to those changes.

Cults seek to replace a lost community and a lost idealism. While it is impossible to speak of cults as a monolithic entity—for there are many kinds, requiring different degrees of commitment—all share certain elements. They offer community, meaning, and spiritual direction, serving as ad hoc rites of passage in a society where traditional institutions seem to be failing. Yet, whereas socially sanctioned rites of passage are temporary arrangements that lead to the acquisition of new roles and new status within the larger society, cults exist on the fringe of society, neither outlawed nor fully accepted. They are not subject to control by the larger group, and many of them do not want to reintegrate their members back into the larger group—quite the reverse. They deliberately maintain members in a kind of limbo, permanently suspended from the surrounding environment.

A critical question, then, is, How widespread is the cult phenomenon? How many people actually belong to cults? What is the real power of these organizations? How much of a danger do they pose to the established social fabric? These questions are hard to answer. They require facts, figures, and an objectivity that is often nonexistent. The cults, on the one hand, are often unwilling to share information about their memberships, wealth, and activities. Moreover, they have an ax to grind; they are seeking to establish their legitimacy and to quell any criticism of their practices. On the other hand, the accounts of ex-members cannot be regarded as perfectly objective. They too have a personal stake in the subject, as do, so often, the "cult watchers"—the deprogrammers, parents, journalists, mental-health professionals, and lawyers who follow cults. The charged atmosphere surrounding cults makes it difficult to establish an accurate picture of the phenomenon.

Estimates of cult memberships, for example, range wildly from the thousands to the millions, depending in large part on what is considered a "cult." When groups like Jehovah's Witnesses or the Mormon Church are included, as some estimates do, the figures soar. A frequently cited estimate is that of Flo Conway and Jim Siegelman, authors of *Snapping*, who maintain that there are 3 million past and present cult members in the United States today. Other common estimates indicate that the Church of Scientology has 4 million members worldwide; the Unification Church, 2 million worldwide; the Divine Light Mission, 1.2 million worldwide; and Hare Krishna (International Society for Krishna Consciousness, or ISKCON), between 10,000 and 12,000 members in the United States, with hundreds of thousands more in India and the rest of the world.[3]

The Gallup Youth Survey came up with somewhat different figures. The survey polled teenagers in 1978 and 1981 about their religious views. Based on an estimate that there are 25 million teenagers in the United States, Gallup projected the following figures in response to the question, "Which, if any, of these [new religious movements] are you involved in or do you practice?"

	1978		1981	
Charismatic Renewal	2%	(500,000)	2.3%	(575,000)
Unification Church	1%	(250,000)	1.6%	(400,000)
Eastern religions	3%	(750,000)	5.9%	(1,475,000)
Bible study	27%	(6,750,000)	40.9%	(10,225,000)
Hare Krishna	1%	(250,000)	1.5%	375,000)
Total	34%	(8,500,000)	52.2%	(13,050,000)

Note: The standard of error for 1,000 is 2 percent near the 10 percent range; 4 percent near the 90 percent range.

Gallup's figures regarding Hare Krishna and the Unification Church as well as other frequently cited estimates are puzzling, for although they included fully participating members as well as people only peripherally involved—attending occasional meetings or classes—most indications are that these groups, along with Scientology and Divine Light Mission, have been experiencing a declining membership.

Curious about the discrepancy, I called a few of these groups and asked their public relations spokesmen for membership figures. The Hare Krishna employee first referred to the 1978 Gallup Youth Survey that indicated 1 percent or a projected 250,000 teenagers were involved in the group. When I pressed the question, requesting a breakdown between full-time or "staff" members who devoted themselves entirely to the group, and part-time members who attended services without any necessary regularity, the picture changed. I was told that there were 5,000 full-time members in the United States, and that full-time membership was "waning a bit."

I had virtually the same conversation with the Scientologists. The first figures cited were expansive: 3 million members in the United States and between 5 and 6 million members worldwide. However, full-time membership in the United States—that is, accountable membership—was only 6,500.

The same situation holds for Sun Myung Moon's Unification Church. Despite the church's claims of 37,000 members in the United States (a far cry from Gallup's 1981 figure of 400,000), many cult watchers feel that actual membership is more like one-tenth of what the church claims. Galen Kelly, a deprogrammer who has worked extensively with members of the Unification Church and who, given his profession, might have an interest in inflating the "danger," believes that 4,000 United States citizens are members of the church, and that there are a few thousand foreign members in the country as well. Robert Boettcher, whose book, *Gifts of Deceit*, explores the connection between the Unification Church and the Korean CIA, and who served on the House subcommittee that investigated that connection, estimates that there are under 5,000 Moonies in the United States today.

These figures also present a misleading impression of the cult phenomenon. They do not take into consideration the large numbers of "part-time" members who contribute substantial amounts of time and money to their respective groups; and they do not give any indication of the potential market for similar groups. The Gallup Youth Survey testifies to the enormous spiritual hunger of young people today. Despite discrepancies in figures of cult memberships, it is clear that a large proportion of teenagers have religious concerns: 95 percent say they believe in God; 68 percent say that they have had the feeling of being in God's presence. Yet over one-third of those who describe themselves as "very religious" do not attend church.[4] Moreover, it is possible that the largest proportion of people involved in cults belong to groups so small as to go unnoticed by the general public. Between five hundred and two thousand such groups exist today.

The real power of these groups, in any case, is a function not merely of their membership rolls, but also of their economic assets and resources. Here, too, accurate appraisals are difficult to obtain, for churches are not obliged to fully disclose their finances; nevertheless, realization of the wealth of some of the larger organizations is inescapable. According to the House Subcommittee on International Relations, the Unification Church's real estate holdings in this country are worth upward of $200 million. In the New York City area alone, the church's holdings are estimated at over $75 million and include the former New Yorker Hotel and the former Tiffany Building.[5] Hare Krishna owns two dozen urban properties, including a fourteen-story temple/residence in Manhattan. Two small portions of Synanon's California real estate holdings that it put up for sale were valued respectively at $7 million and $1.5 million. The Way International owns property in seven states, including two colleges, a family ranch, and a camp, which has an estimated worth of about $8 million. Scientology recently paid $8 million for properties in Clearwater, Florida, its current headquarters.[6]

Real estate holdings are just one indication of the wealth of these organizations; their income is generated from diverse sources. ISKCON, for example, reported in a property tax suit an annual income of $762,208 from panhandling in Los Angeles alone.[7] Scientology's net worth has been estimated by lawyer Michael Flynn, whose Boston firm has filed a class-action suit against the church, at over $400 million. Much of Scientology's income is generated from self-help courses it offers, which range from $150 to $350 per hour, with the average Scientologist spending about $5,000, and a few, up to $100,000. One former Scientologist administrator claims that the Clearwater branch grosses as much as $1 million a week.[8] The church also earns income from twenty-two private children's schools (the Apple Schools) located around the country.

The income of the Unification Church, whose businesses are probably the most diversified, is estimated at between $109 and $219 million a year. While the church admits to raising $20 to $25 million annually from street sales of flowers, candy, and other trifles, University of Texas sociologist Anson Shupe believes, based on his research of the group, that the real figure is more like $30 to $50 million. Apart from monies raised from soliciting, church profits come from a fishing industry, art galleries, a Korean armaments-manufacturing plant and a pharmaceutical company, a ginseng business, restaurants, a publishing business (which includes a printing company in San Francisco and English and Spanish daily newspapers in New York City), and a rug-cleaning business. In addition, the Unification Church produced the film *Inchon*, a $42-million Korean War epic, and obtained, at least temporarily, a controlling interest in the Diplomat National Bank in Washington, D.C.

Before its violent collapse, the People's Temple was also rich. After the deaths in Guyana, it was disclosed that Jones had stashed away over $10 million in various bank accounts. Most of that money came from temple members who had turned over to their leader possessions, pensions, and social security checks.

Any assessment of the cult phenomenon must also establish its parameters, for the term *cult* covers a wide range of disparate groups and organizations. Practically speaking, the groups generally described as cults today share in greater or lesser degree the following attributes: an authoritarian structure, the regimentation of followers, renunciation of the world, and the belief that adherents alone are gifted with the truth. All the other qualities associated with cults derive from these characteristics: an attitude of moral superiority, a contempt for secular laws, rigidity of thought, and the diminution of regard for the individual.

Cults can be categorized by the intensity of control they exert over their members, as well as by their ideological content. At one end of the intensity scale are the *totalistic* cults, which attempt to control the total environment of individual followers. Most totalistic cults advocate complete withdrawal from the world, condemning those outside as "ungodly" or "satanic." These groups put tremendous pressure on members to conform completely to the group, to sever all ties with the past, and to give up any independent thoughts or actions. The Unification Church and Hare Krishna are both examples of totalistic cults. Their followers are strictly regimented—living together, working together, and praying together, each day's activities dictated by the group.

A key in determining the degree of control the group exercises over its members is the amount of time spent in mind-altering activities—prayer, chanting, meditation, group rituals, psychodrama, and confession, for these activities effectively isolate members from the outside world. A survey of four hundred ex-cult members from forty-eight different groups revealed an average time of fifty-five hours per week spent in activities of this type.[9] Members of Hare Krishna spend the most time in ritual and indoctrination sessions—some seventy hours per week, with most members chanting seven hours a day.

Another important distinction must be made between groups that are live-in organizations and those that are not. Generally speaking, groups that are not live-in have less control over their members. Some groups, such as Scientology, The Way International, and Hare Krishna, have two levels of membership: full-time, live-in members and part-time, out-of-house members. Part-time ISKCON members attend some functions, but their lives are not as dominated by the group. Scientology is similarly organized and can be considered to be a totalistic cult for those "staff" members who live together and whose lives are strictly controlled by the organization. Most members, however, live and work independently but attend Scientology's "auditing" sessions, which are confessional-like courses that promise to liberate the mind and body.

Freedom of movement varies from cult to cult. Some cults, such as the Unification Church, maintain security forces, which, along with protecting the group, prevent members from freely coming and going. Divine Light Mission can be described as a middle-range cult. Although members spend large amounts of time meditating, most live outside the "ashram" and are free to come and go as they choose. More "devoted" members live together, and it is probable that they are as dominated by the group as are the members of the more clearly totalistic groups.

Moreover, the different branches of the same cult may vary in the degree of control they exercise over members, and the structure and organization of any one cult may change over time. The People's Temple, in its twenty years, could not even be described as a cult, but was a Protestant church with a charismatic leader. Over time, as Jones developed a grandiose vision of himself and began to demand sacrifices from his followers, the nature of his organization began to change. A hierarchy developed, replacing what had once been a loosely structured, egalitarian group, and the freedom of his followers was gradually curtailed. At first members of Jones's congregation were free to come and go as they pleased and were not required to renounce the outside world in any way, but by the time the group reached Guyana, Jonestown had become a prison ruled by a messiah whose word was law.

Most of the groups just described are religious cults. ISKCON and Divine Light derive from Asian religious teachings, while the Unification Church is part of a Christian tradition. Despite calling itself a church, Scientology, in fact, is more akin to the other great genre of cults, the therapy cults, which come out of the human-potential movement.

One of the oldest cults, Scientology was founded by the science-fiction writer L. Ron Hubbard in 1954 and based on the science of "Dianetics." According to the "science," man is plagued by "engrams," the mental images resulting from painful experiences in the past—either from this life or from former incarnations. Engrams can be "cleared" through "auditing," a process whereby a Scientology minister locates a person's engrams and clears them for $150 an hour. The auditing procedure consists of having the subject grip two empty tin cans wired to a battery-powered galvanometer. The auditor asks the subject a variety of questions about his or her past and present lives. The needle's fluctuations indicate where there are engrams, which the person is then forced to confront. Auditors claim in this way to help individuals to "clear the memory bin," thus liberating their minds and bodies.[10]

Scientology and the other therapeutic cults frame the salvation they offer in psychological terms, as personal liberation or cure. These groups are what anthropologists call "cults of affliction." Membership is precipitated by illness, and once cured, the formerly afflicted graduate becomes the priest of a new generation of sufferers.

Although some of the therapeutic cults do not claim to be

religious organizations, their techniques are not all that different from those practiced by the Unification Church or ISKCON. Prayer in the Unification Church, auditing in Scientology, "exercises" in *est*, and confronting one's "grail" or greatest fear in Lifespring are all intense forms of confession. Combined with mind-altering techniques—chanting, hypnotic training routines, talking in tongues—and in the context of group pressure, they constitute a form of conditioning to break down the individual. In each of these groups, submission to the group is characterized as the height of personal liberation and transcendence. Once achieved, transcendence creates a feeling of shared experience and superiority that binds members of the group.

What is most disturbing to many critics of cults is that the groups represent a form of social contract alien to an open, democratic society. What proponents of cults consider to be spiritual or psychological expansion is seen by others as the deliberate subversion of the individual's will and autonomy. Particularly since the mass deaths in Jonestown, the cult issue has become bitterly controversial. The despair of parents whose children have joined cults has been exacerbated and dramatized by that tragedy. Many have resorted to extreme and often illegal methods to extricate their children from the clutches of the cults. The cults, on the other hand, feel they have been marked for persecution, that the very label *cult* is a pejorative one that denies them legitimacy. In consequence, a major confrontation exists, with psychiatrists, religious leaders, professional deprogrammers, parents, and jurists positioned in fixed ranks against the cults.

Cults do warrant close scrutiny. They force us to examine many of our unspoken assumptions about the society in which we live. This book concentrates on the practices of the more extreme cults, precisely because they provide the clearest examples of the changed relationships between the individual and his social group. Given the existing spiritual hunger in the United States at this time, these changes have important implications for the future of our society.

2 ≡

SOCIAL MYTHS
AND FAIRY TALES

Human beings need order. They need a framework that can account for and explain experience. In large measure, this framework is provided by social institutions that organize and regulate different aspects of reality. Kinship institutions, for example, establish a group's expectations of, and obligations to, one another. They determine who is and who is not part of this group, who may and who may not marry, whether a married couple live together and where, and which people inherit what from each other.

Religion and social mythology preside over a less tangible realm of experience. They help make the unknowable understandable. Death, fate, and misfortune are conceptualized and explained, at least in part, by social myths that describe the relation between events, human beings, and the supernatural world. For example, among the tribal Azande of the Sudan, if a house collapses and a man is crushed beneath it, his family is not satisfied by knowing that their kinsman's death was caused by a combination of rotting timbers, soil erosion, and a heavy rainfall. These facts are recognized, but they do not ultimately explain why the house fell at one moment rather than at another, or why it fell when one man and not another was in it. What we would be prone to dismiss as coincidence, the Azande attribute to supernatural forces. Witches, they believe, were responsible for the death of their kinsman. By including the dimension of intent in causal explanations, the Azande bestow meaning and significance upon events and experience. In consequence, they experience their universe as better ordered and more controllable.

Social myths not only make experience understandable, they help to shape it. In an interesting account of childbirth among the Cuna Indians of the Republic of Panama, the anthropologist Claude Lévi-Strauss describes the process of curing a woman who is unable to deliver normally. A ritual specialist or shaman is called in to assist her, and his cure consists of a long narrative. The shaman never actually touches his patient; rather, the narrative itself provides a bridge to her physical experience. The shaman explains the events that necessitated his intervention, and describes his subsequent "journey" to the home of the spirit responsible for the trouble. This descriptive journey is, in essence, an allegorical rendering of the physical sensations of the afflicted woman. The spirit Muu and her abode represent the vagina and the uterus; they are spiritual personifications of anatomical organs. And the monsters the shaman encounters en route to Muu's dwelling place—the octopus whose sticky tentacles are alternately opening and closing, the tigers with huge claws that rip and tear things—are mythological embodiments of real sensations. As Lévi-Strauss notes, the shaman's itinerary is a true mythical anatomy, which corresponds to a kind of emotional geography within the patient.[1] During the course of the narration, physical sensation and fiction merge, and the patient begins to identify her experience with the story being told her. This identification in turn creates in her a physiological susceptibility—myth begins to shape experience.

At the beginning of the tale, for example, the shaman and his helpers enter Muu's abode single file; at the end, they depart in rows of four. The purpose of these details is to elicit an organic reaction, but, as Lévi-Strauss points out, "the sick woman could not integrate it as experience if it were not associated with a true increase in dilation." [2] The cure, in short, occurs in the process of translating inchoate experience into a form accessible to the conscious mind and amenable to action.

The need for order, as the Cuna example illustrates, is physiological as well as intellectual. Experiments in sensory restriction indicate the extent of our dependency on order or meaningful information. These experiments are of two types: those that eliminate sensation, such as the classic "sensory deprivation" experiment in which a blindfolded subject is suspended in a tank of water; and those that eliminate the meaning of sensation, or "pattern deprivation" experiments, in which the subject receives sensory input but is deprived of the information needed to make sense of it. These experiments have shown that when the ordinary flow of sensory information is disrupted, behavior becomes disturbed, often to the point of psychosis. The water-tank experiments have typically resulted in delusions, hallucinations, heightened suggestibility, and persuadability.

Experiments in sensory restriction provide a dramatic analogy to what individuals undergo during periods of widespread social upheaval. When the environment becomes unstable, people lose the informational anchors that help them interpret experience. They become disoriented. Like the subjects of sensory restriction experiments, they too become more susceptible to persuasion and suggestibility.

The millenarian vision crops up at just such times of disorientation. Kin to a whole genre of social mythology that augments or replaces ordinary explanation, it comes into play during periods of social and personal breakdown, when the complex fabric of institutions, beliefs, and expectations that constitute reality is torn asunder.

The millenarian vision is frequently found in societies that share or have been exposed to Judeo-Christian beliefs. It is clearly not a vision compatible with societies that envision the world as constantly changing, cyclically changing, or never changing. It explains why things have changed, who is responsible, and what should be done. Though the details of each millenarian vision vary, the basic scenario remains the same. Good and Evil meet in ultimate battle; Good prevails through Divine intervention, and a new world emerges, freed from the Evil that beset the old, and ruled by the Saved, who will reign happily ever after.

In many ways, the millenarian vision plays a role for adults similar to that of fairy tales for children. A comparison between the two sheds light on how such a simple fantasy can mobilize grown people into seemingly bizarre cults and movements.

Fairy tales, as Bruno Bettelheim has shown, are invaluable to the psychological growth of children. They are a kind of symbolic language that gives external form to inner experience. Though often violent, they possess the intrinsic safety of all theater, and they are hedged by an unchanging formula that begins "Once upon a time . . ." and ends ". . . happily ever after." Within the comfort of those limitations, all sorts of psychological mayhem breaks loose. Parents are killed off, stepmothers shoved in ovens, grandmothers devoured, and siblings betrayed.

Children live in a world governed by giants, all-powerful, all-knowing giants whose rules are often hard to ascertain and whose good will is so critical. The child is involved in a constant struggle to make sense out of an external world that is beyond his comprehending, and he is beset by fears, jealousies, needs, and drives that he can neither understand nor fully express. Infancy is a time of explosive angers and frustrations, of nameless emotions colliding with one another without warning or transition.

The violence of fairy tales suits the psyche of a child. The stories ride that thin line between inner and outer reality, giving tangible form to amorphous, inarticulate emotions. The images in fairy tales, in essence, are symbolic figures that correspond to a shifting emotional reality, a kind of psychological kaleidoscope whose elements assume new meaning within the constantly changing context of the developing child. But the preamble "Once upon a time . . ." cautions the child that the story is not to be confused with real life.

Most of the stories have to do with Oedipal jealousies, revenge, sibling rivalry, and the terrors of dependence. They all concern power: the power to outwit those who are stronger and more cunning, the power to triumph over seemingly insurmountable odds. Most of the victories in fairy tales, though they are utterly predictable within the genre, are totally unrealistic: Hansel and Gretel, mere children, defeat the wicked witch; poor, despised Cinderella wins the hand of the Prince; the youngest, weakest, stupidest son of the King succeeds where his cleverer brothers have failed and wins the throne.

Fairy tales acknowledge the helplessness the child feels, for the hero is usually an unassuming, powerless person set loose in a world populated by witches, looming monsters, enormous, impenetrable castles, and conniving animals. He or she is assigned an impossible task. Realistically, the hero and heroine cannot be expected to succeed. Yet somehow, miraculously, they do, almost invariably thanks to a miracle or magical intervention: the fairy godmother outfits Cinderella; magic animals protect and aid the hero or heroine. Thus the prevailing message of fairy tales, despite the terrifying world they conjure, is one of monumental hope and promise.

The millenarian vision is surprisingly similar. It depicts a dangerous, evil world, which, like that of the fairy tales, is peopled with "creatures" of superhuman proportions. "And I stood upon the sand of the sea and saw a beast rise up out of the sea, having ten horns. And it was given to him to make war with the saints, and to overcome them; and power was given to him over all kindreds, and tongues, and nations. . . . And I beheld another beast coming up out of the earth. And he doeth great wonders and deceiveth them that dwell on the earth by means of those miracles which he has power to do." [3] This description is not from a fairy tale, but rather the prototypic millenarian vision from the Book of Daniel.

As narrative, the millenarian vision is peculiar. For despite the violent content of the vision, it is related in a flat, passive voice. Events occur, they are not actively brought about. The Saved inherit the earth as though watching the event on television. This passivity in part can be explained by the fact that the events described are the consequence of Divine powers that transpire at a level removed from the common herd. Yet there is another aspect to it, as well. The odd juxtaposition of neutrality and violence expresses a state of mind.

The millenarian fantasy appeals to people whose world has suddenly overturned, who find themselves in familiar surroundings that no longer make sense. Even the ground underfoot has become suspect, liable to slide or lurch without warning. Cult followers are people whose expectations have been thwarted. They feel cheated and resentful but either are too disoriented to cope with the situation or are excluded from the legitimate avenues of redress. The claustrophobia of impending doom so vividly depicted in the messianic vision describes this sense of ubiquitous threat and its passive quality, the loss of control.

This sense of impotence also permeates children's fairy tales. Left to herself, Cinderella is smaller than life, diminutive in comparison with her loud stepmother and brash stepsisters. Magic bestows upon her the dimensions of a heroine. She is transformed by a magical costume and coach whose glitter is sadly short-lived.

In messianic tales, ultimate triumph also occurs through Divine intervention. The faithful, if they act at all, do so almost as an afterthought. Their usual role is to prepare themselves for the Great Day—to perform the appropriate rituals, to purify themselves, and to wait. Cargo Cult followers abandoned their villages, retiring to the hills to await the millennium; Ghost Dance devotees danced themselves into utter exhaustion in preparation for the Final Judgment. These examples are hardly unique. Not too long ago, Jim Jones exhorted his disciples to ready themselves:

> I have seen, by divine revelation, the total annihilation of this country and other parts of the world. San Francisco will be flattened. The only survivors will be those people who are hidden in the caves that I have been shown in a vision. Those who go into this cave with me will be saved from the poisonous radioactive fallout that will follow the nuclear bomb attack. This cave is what led our church to migrate to this little valley from Indianapolis, Indiana. . . . We have gathered in Redwood Valley for protection, and after the war is over we will be the only survivors. It will be up to our group to begin life anew on this

continent. Then we will begin a truly ideal society. . . . People will care about one another. Elderly people will be made to feel needed and will be allowed to be productive. . . . There will at last be peace on earth. I have seen this all by divine revelation.[4]

None of these groups pictured itself as actively bringing about the millennium. They did not take up arms, but instead retreated, in one form or another, from the real world.

Some groups, though, are more passive than others. Melanesians under colonial rule and North American Indians in the last century would have been suicidal to have framed their vision in more aggressive terms. The Mormons, on the other hand, were openly antagonistic, but even they were vague about the actual mechanism of the final confrontation. They warned their neighbors that it was imminent, and they went so far as to engage in petty thievery and combat. Yet they never actually elaborated on their vision of the millennium.

The sense of impotence in both messianic and fairy tales is underscored by the generic quality of the protagonists. The Saved remain faceless and nameless. In fairy tales too, as Bettelheim points out,

> Typical titles are "Beauty and the Beast," "The Fairy Tale of One Who Went Forth to Learn Fear."
> . . . If names appear, it is quite clear that these are not proper names, but general or descriptive ones. We are told that "Because she always looked dusty and dirty, they called her Cinderella," or: "A little red cap suited her so well that she was always called "Little Red Cap." [5]

In millenarian tales, the protagonists are not fully drawn characters, but stereotypes. If anything, the Saved are more vaguely described than the Damned. The latter are at least colorful, attributed with the characteristics of despised groups within the culture. In the millenarian vision of the Third Reich, for example, the Damned had hooked noses and jingling pockets. In Ayatollah Khomeini's movement, Western dress, education, and customs constitute telltale signs of Satanic poison. The image of Satan, in short, is malleable, a cutout doll upon whom specific attributes can be imposed, lending itself to all sorts of projections and identifications.

There is a difference, however, between the characterization in millenarian visions and that in fairy tales. The child's need for revenge, for winning against formidable enemies, must remain secret, and the evil stepmothers and witches anonymous. The child himself is not conscious of his own projections. To recognize or name these adversaries would create intolerable conflict, for they are simultaneously adversaries and loved ones. The value of the fairy tale is that it allows for the expression of anger and resentment in a permissible way. Anonymity protects both the child and the objects of his anger. The followers of a messianic cult, however, need not refrain from naming their enemies. Unlike the child, they are not intimately bound up with or dependent on the objects of their wrath, so the targeting of their anger is cathartic. Thus in the millenarian vision, Satan often has a distinct name and identity.

Revenge is at the heart of these stories. And it is a neat, symmetrical revenge: the wolf in Little Red Riding Hood (Little Red Cap) has his belly sewn up with rocks; Hansel and Gretel's witch ends up in the oven; the white trespassers in Melanesia are drowned in the sea from which they so mysteriously arrived. The revenge is childlike, without mercy. Roles are simply reversed, the bullied become bullies. Red Riding

Hood does not attempt to rehabilitate the wolf, put a little leash on him, and take him for nature walks.

The happy endings of fairy tales confirm the simplicity of their vision, yet they are oddly empty. The Kingdom won, at the end of the story, like the millenarian dream, is nondescript. Its main characteristic, according to Bettelheim, is that

> we are never told anything about it, not even what the king or queen does. There is no purpose to being the king or queen of this kingdom other than being a ruler rather than the ruled. To have become a king or queen at the conclusion of the story symbolizes a state of true independence, in which the hero feels so secure, satisfied, and happy, as the infant in his most dependent state, when he was truly well taken care of in the kingdom of his cradle.[6]

In the millenarian Kingdom, the Saved live in a paradise on earth where "there shall be no more death, neither sorrow nor crying, neither shall there be any more pain: for the former things are passed away." [7] How they live, how they rule, and what ruling entails is conspicuously absent in these tales. All we are told is that the previously existing power relations have been reversed. It is assumed that merely having the power that has been so long denied will bring happiness.

The reunion with dead ancestors and the eradication of death altogether figure strongly in many millenarian visions and parallel Bettelheim's appraisal of fairy tales as a metaphorical return to infancy. For here too separation is abolished forever—one is never alone again.

In a simple way, both fairy tales and messianic visions are accounts of wishful thinking—about getting even, achieving power, being loved and protected. As the vagueness of their goals reveals, they are not strategies for practical behavior, but fantasies in which the desired wish irrationally comes about.

In the fairy tale, this vagueness is understandable. The child has no idea of what is actually involved in being a king or queen (the symbols of successful adulthood), except that it is desirable. The outside world is imagined as a gigantic projection of family life, and the exotic adventures of fairy tales are nothing more than the thinly camouflaged exploration of those intimate relationships.

The messianic fantasy, however, pertains to adults, not children, yet the world view it projects is that of a child. The security promised is the reward for complete dependence on a glorified father who rules his Kingdom with supreme, if benevolent, authority. Here too paradise is envisioned as a family.

There is false modesty in this vision of the world, for although all power and authority are vested in a remote father, he is perceived as totally absorbed by the doings of his children. One's need to feel as though one were the center of the universe reveals an insecurity about the real position one occupies in the world. It is a common phenomenon among children who have no other status outside of the family.

The size of the world and one's place in it seem inversely proportionate to the degree of personal security one feels. The peculiar mixture of humility and egocentrism is nowhere more evident than in fairy tales where the monumental size ascribed to adversaries reflects simultaneously the child's sense of being overwhelmed by the world and his own ultimate place at its center. The radical fluctuations of perceived size from invisible to gigantic—best described in *Alice in Wonderland*—express the distorted perspective of children whose relationship to the outside world is so uncertain.

The need to be larger than life, to be embarked on an all-important, earth-shaking mission (to compensate for the lowly or unsatisfactory status occupied in real life) is critical to the followers of messianic movements. They jealously guard their role as Elect, for it is in this role that they have managed to accept and reintegrate themselves in "reality." Their identity is tentative, hinged on the exaggerated proportions of Satan.

For adults, the concept of the millennium as an eternal, happy family constitutes a violent step backward. Here, unlike Alice, who grows and diminishes in relation to others, the world itself shrinks to become a tottering stage on which enormous heroes act out carefully rehearsed parts. Despite the magnitude of their proportions, the players are only stick figures, the stock symbols of a morality play: Good and Evil, Christ and Antichrist, the Saved and the Damned.

The fantasy reflects an overwhelming need to make the world manageable again. It succeeds by isolating confusing aspects of experience and treating them as though they were discrete entities. Evil is projected onto scapegoats who become its symbols. At various times and to various groups in twentieth-century America, Communists, Jews, Bankers, Atheists, Zionists, the British, and the Eastern Aristocracy have been as instantly recognizable as the wolf in children's fairy stories. Ambiguity is so intolerable that unacceptable aspects of the self are magically eliminated by this process of separation and projection. Believers in the messianic vision reject those parts of themselves that threaten their new identity. Moonies, for example, attribute any doubts about the Unification Church to the pernicious intrusion of Satan.

The peculiar symmetry between Christ and Antichrist, the Saved and the Damned, is that they are the polar ends of a dialectical vision, each end defined by reference to its opposite. A similar process occurs in fairy tales where complex or ambivalent feelings are split and projected onto distinct images. The division into opposites is a basic human function, as well as a major function of myth. The infant learns to distinguish and identify an object only by learning what it is not. (We have all seen small children who have just mastered recognition of a new object go painstakingly around a room to a variety of different objects, proudly pointing out, in delighted pedagogy, that these are *not* the newly learned object.) Bettelheim writes:

> This is also how the fairy tale depicts the world: figures are ferocity incarnate or unselfish benevolence. An animal is either all-devouring or all-helpful. Every figure is essentially one-dimensional, enabling the child to comprehend its actions and reactions easily. Through simple and direct images the fairy story helps the child sort out his complex and ambivalent feelings, so that these begin to fall, each one into a separate place, rather than being all one big muddle.[8]

It is also common for children to split the image of a parent into two separate feelings: the good mother, for example, and an entirely different person who just pretends to be the mother. The impostor, unlike the mother, is often angry and critical of the child, behavior that the child cannot comprehend or integrate with the person of his real mother. This device not only resolves intolerable contradictions, but it also alleviates the guilt the child would otherwise feel toward his "good" mother. He is able to direct his anger entirely against the impostor, keeping the good mother inviolate.*

---

* Bettelheim says the "child not only splits a parent into two figures, but he may also split himself into two people, who, he wishes to believe, have nothing in common with each other. I have known young children who during the day are successfully dry but wet their bed at night and, waking up, move with disgust to a corner and say with conviction, 'Somebody's wet my bed.' The child does not do this, as parents may think,

This natural solution is mirrored endlessly in the wicked stepmothers, witches, and good fairy godmothers of fairy tales. The dreadful ends many "bad" parents meet in these stories are wholly satisfying, for they involve neither guilt nor responsibility. Fairy tales are pointedly make-believe, and all mayhem is vicarious. The child need never consciously realize just why fairy tales are so compelling.

The messianic vision also manages to legitimize antisocial feelings. And like the fairy tale, it absolves its followers of responsibility. The revenge depicted in the vision is considered to be fated by God. The followers, who certainly benefit at the expense of the Damned, absolve themselves from any guilt through their pervasive passivity. By projecting their own desires onto a God who then takes matters into his own hands, they manage to satisfy their need for revenge and remain morally impeccable.

Both messianic visions and fairy tales occupy that peculiar mythical space at the edge of the psyche and speak a language that is neither exclusively internal monologue nor external discourse, but both simultaneously. They are symbolic narratives that create a context for the examination and articulation of certain problems. They are fables that concern, among other things, identity and dependence. They use similar psychological and mental processes because a similar state of mind has made them necessary in the first place.

The child and the follower of the messianic vision feel over-

to put the blame on somebody else, knowing all the while that it was he who urinated in the bed. The 'somebody' who has done it is that part of himself with which he has by now parted company; this aspect of his personality has actually become a stranger to him." This is almost identical to the adult who denies certain aspects of himself as the intrusion of an outside evil force, thus preserving his self-image by eradicating all unacceptable feelings.

whelmed by the world and are struggling to understand and integrate themselves into it. Both, for different reasons, lack grounding—a solid connectedness and sense of place in reality. Messianic visions and fairy tales are the fragile attempts to cope. The child's only sure link to the outside world is through his family, which is why, even when the fairy tale climaxes with the achievement of independence, independence can only be imagined in familial terms. The adult, disappointed in a reality that has not lived up to his expectations, projects, in the messianic vision, a solution that also symbolizes a return to the family. But where the child is hopeful, identifying adulthood with happiness and success, the follower of the messianic vision fantasizes about becoming a child again.

Nor does the fairy tale attempt to foist itself off as reality. It makes sure, by way of cautionary preambles, that the child realizes that the story is make-believe. In fact, by disclaiming any relation to reality, the fairy tale frees the listener to project, identify, and fantasize without inhibition. It allows the child to enjoy revenge and vindication without the burden of guilt, for the fairy tale insists that it is nothing more than entertainment.

The messianic vision, on the other hand, asserts that it is an accurate representation of reality, and it insulates its followers from any other. Given the rigidity of its vision, it is not liberating but doctrinaire and dangerous. It is one thing to suggest, by way of parable, that anger is legitimate and justifiable. It is another to imply that this anger may be legitimately acted out without qualms of conscience.

Both the messianic vision and the fairy tale offer hope as well as a wonderful new identity. But here too, despite similarities, they are at cross purposes. The fairy tale gives the child courage to explore the world and to discover a place for himself in it by reducing the world and its inhabitants to manageable, one-dimensional proportions. This device is constructive in the context of a child's limited ability to perceive and comprehend. It is anything but, in the context of adult listeners. The simplistic vision of the messianic prophecy would make most adults blush—a world inhabited by Good people and Bad people, with nothing in between. Even the individual has been eliminated. All that is left is a group identity, for the self has been effaced, ostensibly for the Cause. At the end of the fairy tale, the hero becomes an individual, a successful adult who happily rules his kingdom. The child, in the fairy tale and in the natural course of life, succeeds his parent. In the messianic vision, he doesn't, and instead returns to the childhood fold where adulthood, like some hideous burden, is thankfully abdicated for ever after.

3 ≡

THE MESSIAHS

Upon scrutiny, the leaders of cults in America today fit into the classic messianic pattern, whether or not they frame the salvation they offer in traditional religious terms. While many contemporary "messiahs" offer programs in personal and psychological self-help, the ideological nature of these "programs" reveals their messianic character: these are not mere therapies designed to ameliorate or cope with problems, but cures for total salvation that, if adhered to, will radically transform the lives of their practitioners.

A messiah is a savior, an expected deliverer, the emissary of God sent to save the world from imminent ruin. The messiah is an expression of hope and desperation, a figure almost of fantasy, who materializes when all appears to be lost. Messiahs arrive on the brink of disaster proffering instant salvation. Their vision is absolutist, their promises as well: absolute redemption, absolute fulfillment in exchange for absolute loyalty. It is, in fact, this quality of absoluteness that is their hallmark.

Ironically, though, most messiahs have had markedly unstable lives. Their backgrounds and life histories are rife with traumatic experiences. It is commonplace among them that their calling is precipitated by crisis, nervous breakdown, and physical collapse. Most messiahs are people who have been unable to successfully integrate themselves into ordinary society. They are marginal individuals—members of groups denied access to power, or individuals who for a variety of reasons have failed to achieve it. As a group, messiahs also display other characteristics. They are ambitious, intelligent, and rigid; thus, despite their inability to follow the usual routes to success, they manage to create their own.

One of the first and best-known of the twentieth-century messiahs was George Baker, better known as Father Divine. Divine's path was simple. Basically an entrepreneur, he became a spiritual leader because other roads to success within the white and black middle classes were closed to him. And if one thing marked the career of Divine, it was the burning desire to be recognized, to be important.

In becoming a messiah, Divine was not breaking new ground but following a long and established tradition among his race and social class. Religion had long been a natural arena for social mobility among blacks, for it was one of the few areas where intelligence and drive brought high rewards. While middle-class blacks gravitated toward the established ministries, men like Baker—emigrants from the rural South—were more inclined to street-corner pulpits. Harlem, especially after the great migration from the South during the World War I period, was filled with idiosyncratic churches and messiahs. Divine was one among many. His success must be attributed to a mixture of opportune events and his own shrewd sense of human needs.

Divine was born near the Savannah River toward the end of the nineteenth century. He left at an early age and traveled north to Baltimore. There he became the apprentice of Samuel Morris, a preacher at the Baptist Church Colored. Morris fancied himself a messiah and appointed Divine to be his assistant, dubbing him the Messenger in the Sonship Degree.

By 1914, Divine had learned all he could from Morris. He left Baltimore and next turned up in Valdosta, Georgia, on trial in the case of *John Doe alias God* v. *the State of Georgia*. He was accused of stirring up the hardworking citizens of Valdosta, especially the women, causing them to run through the streets declaring that God had arrived and to talk belligerently of throwing off their yoke of bondage. The court found Divine guilty, declared him a public nuisance, and asked him to leave the state. He did, taking a few of his converts with him.

Divine moved from town to town, preaching and picking up converts until he eventually reached Brooklyn, where he settled with his flock. He leased a house on Myrtle Avenue and set up communal housekeeping. As God, he was naturally the head of the house. He found jobs for his "children," as he called his disciples, took charge of their earnings, and made sure they were well fed and the rent was paid. On Sundays, outsiders were invited to the Myrtle Avenue home, where they were treated to a huge feast and stirring sermon.

By 1919, the Myrtle Avenue house was overflowing. Divine found new quarters for his flock in the white middle-class neighborhood of Sayville, Long Island.

Divine ran his ménage with a firm hand. He was its sole authority and he did his utmost to seal it off from the rest of the world. Although members worked on the outside, they were forbidden to have relationships with outsiders, even if those included members of their own families. Divine dismissed family members with a typical flourish: "God," he proclaimed, "is your father, your mother, your sister, and your brother, and you never had another." He banned from his commune sex, money, and acknowledgment of race. As far as he was concerned, these "evils" simply did not exist.

The emotional dependence of his followers was underscored by their economic dependence. Divine went out of his way to court people with money and possessions. After the convert joined, his or her assets went into the communal coffer, over which Divine presided. All earnings were also garnered by Divine, who redistributed them as he saw fit.

The consequences of such all-encompassing dependence were predictable. Many couples who had entered the commune together found their marriages disintegrating. They no longer shared a common economic interest; they were forbidden to have sex together; and they were pressured to renounce their families, including their children. In Divine's Kingdom, the only legitimate relationship was that between the convert and his "Father."

Divine enjoyed a modest success in Sayville. His Sunday feasts open to outsiders were renowned, and by 1928 he had ninety full-time disciples. It was during the Depression, however, that he achieved real fame and power. His rise, like his early beginnings, was the result of a trial, of notoriety, and of hard times.

In 1931, after buying another Sayville property, Divine and his followers were arrested as a public nuisance and put on trial. His crime was not so much that his Kingdom was a nuisance to the citizens of Sayville—though it must have been, especially on Sundays when busloads of potential converts jammed the roadways leading to "Heaven"—but that it was racially integrated. Not only did a few white converts reside at the Sayville commune, but still more would come to the Sunday services.

The racist character of the trial attracted unexpected support for Divine from the black intelligentsia (which ordinarily disdained street-corner pulpitry) and from the national press, angered by the Scottsboro trial earlier that year. Notwithstanding all the attention, and despite the jury's recommendation of leniency, Divine was found guilty and the judge imposed the maximum sentence. Under ordinary circumstances, that would have been the end of Divine's career, but a bizarre event occurred. Immediately after the sentencing, the judge, despite relative youth and apparent good health, dropped dead. Divine's sentence was reversed on appeal. Thus vindicated, he moved to Harlem, which welcomed him with open arms.

The Depression provided the ideal conditions for Divine's Kingdom. Given a place to sleep, plenty of food, the opportunity to work, and escape from the humiliation of charity, his following soared into the thousands. Divine gave even more to his "children." He instilled in them a sense of pride many had never known. "You are as good as anybody you work for, and your belief in yourself will cause you to be just as you see yourselves to be," he lectured them. The only unpardonable sin in Divine's commune was independent thought. It threatened Divine's rule, and he conveniently rejected it as an obstacle to true worthiness and happiness. With the Depression howling at the gates, this seemed a small sacrifice indeed.

Within a short time, Divine's Kingdom had become an empire, providing cheap food and housing not only to his flock, but to thousands of paying guests. God, Inc., operated twenty-five restaurants, ten butcher shops, two groceries, and ten cleaning stores; it leased three apartment houses and nine private houses; and it operated twenty or thirty itinerant wagons that sold "Peace, Father, Clams, and Oysters." In the depths of the Depression, the Kingdom's weekly take was estimated at $20,000, half of which went for expenses, and half to God.

Father Divine represents one kind of messiah—the messianic entrepreneur. Marginal within his own society, he was forced to create his own. As his personal history gives no indication of psychological disorder or of an inability to successfully manage in the world, but of the reverse, one must deduce that his career as a messiah was largely dictated by external circumstances.

At the other extreme of the messianic spectrum is Jim Jones. He found himself on the fringes of society not because of race, religion, or social class, but because of his personal makeup. He never felt he belonged; he was driven by forces inside him.

Jones consciously emulated Divine, yet he could not have been more different. Where Divine denied the existence of race, whitened photographs of himself, and married a blonde, Jones identified with society's underdogs. He took on the racial issue as a personal cause, not simply defending blacks, but pretending to be black himself.

Jones grew up in Lynn, Indiana. His father, James Thurmond Jones, was a railroad man who was often ailing, having been gassed in World War I. Some assert that the elder Jones was a member of the local Ku Klux Klan, which would make his son's affectations all the more revealing. His mother, according to accounts, was an anthropologist who abandoned her career after dreaming that she would give birth to a son who would save the world. To implement this vision, she married and in 1931 gave birth to Jim Jones.

That young Jim had his problems is evident from available accounts. In Lynn, he is remembered as an unusual boy. His favorite pastime was playing "pretend preacher" to a congregation of other small children. One neighbor recalled that these sermons often included corporal punishment for wayward parishioners. Others remembered the stirring sermons the boy preacher delivered for dead animals, but this too had its perverse side: some neighbors suspected Jim's hand when their cats suddenly disappeared. "We always thought he was using them for sacrifices," one reported.[1]

Cults in America

When he grew older he did become a preacher; his first assignment was with a Methodist church in Indianapolis. He stayed only a few years with the Methodists, however, leaving disillusioned to found a church of his own. Actively engaged in the struggle for civil rights, during his early years Jones channeled his energies outward, toward tangible goals and against real enemies, for his crusading church was often attacked by bigots.

With success, Jones began to degenerate. By the mid- to late 1950s, he had begun skimming the various do-good corporations he had set up, realizing, as he told one friend, that religion was an easy scam. He also became increasingly obsessed with power. A pilgrimage to Father Divine during this period marked a turning point for Jones. Parishioners recall that after this visit he was no longer "Jim" to them, but insisted on being addressed as "Father" or "Dad." He also instituted other changes modeled after Divine's church: he established an interrogation committee to rout out anyone who criticized him and he attempted to limit his followers' contact with the outside world. These developments became entrenched policy over the years.

By 1961, the year he was appointed director of the Indianapolis Human Rights Commission, Jones had begun ranting against the Bible. His associate minister recalls that he once threw a Bible on the floor during a sermon and complained, " 'Too many people are looking at this instead of at me.' He said everybody ought to love him. If they didn't, he'd get awfully violent—not physically, but verbally." Another minister remembered that during this period Jones began to subvert his extraordinary ability to relate to people to get them to do his bidding.

With power lust came paranoia. Jones became obsessed with

the idea of nuclear war, and in 1962 he fled Indianapolis for a remote Brazilian city, which he had read would be one of the nine safest spots in the world in the event of war. He also became a hypochondriac, convinced for the remainder of his life that he was stricken with cancer.

Success, obviously, did not satisfy Jim Jones. His restlessness was not that of a man seeking fresh challenges, but rather that of a man whose own feelings of worthlessness pervaded all his accomplishments. His insecurity caused his emotions to swing from one extreme to the other: at one moment he was God, at another, the scourge of the earth.

By the time he reached Guyana, in 1977, Jones had become crazed by power and paranoia. His idealism, energy, and courage dissipated. What remained of the original man were those elements that had been present in childhood: his ability to persuade others, his sadism, and his fascination with death.

The messiah as entrepreneur, in the case of Father Divine, and the messiah produced by internal combustion, like Jim Jones, represent two extremes of messianic leaders. Yet even these extremes fit into a general class of miracle workers. Saviors, medicine men, shamans—they are called different names in different societies. Notwithstanding cultural and historical differences, the class as a whole is remarkably consistent. It flourishes in periods of social instability; its members are social innovators who confound the established categories and protocols; and they are marginal people in their own societies, viewed simultaneously with awe and distrust.

Of all the varieties of miracle worker, the role of shaman is the most institutionalized and clearly delineated. The recruitment, function, and position of the shaman constitute a pattern whose basic outline is followed by the other miracle workers.

Shamans are religious specialists. The shaman is distinguished from the priest, however, by having a direct line of communication with the supernatural world. He represents what the Caribs of British Honduras have called "a telephone exchange between man and God." But the shaman's relationship with the supernatural world goes beyond simple communication. He is literally possessed by the spirits who enter him and claim him as their own. The anthropologist I. M. Lewis has characterized this relationship as "the seizure of man by divinity." Shamans are those who have been called upon and claimed by the spirits to do their bidding. In exchange, the shaman partakes of their power.

The initial sign of shamanhood is usually manifested as an affliction. A person falls ill and remains ill, impervious to all cures. The sickness abates only after the victim has recognized it as a calling from the spirits. Once the sufferer accepts his fate, he must undertake to learn his craft—to communicate with the spirits and, to some degree, to control them.

Many societies have two distinct types of shamans: hereditary shamans, who have inherited the role, and charismatic shamans, who have been endowed with a divine gift or power. For the latter, the call is a traumatic event that often involves what we would characterize as a severe nervous disorder.

In an account of the life histories of contemporary female Korean shamans, Youngsook Kim Harvey relates that in each case, the illness that signaled the calling was preceded by personal trauma: the death of a child, relocation to a new environment, the inability to conceive. For these women, becoming a shaman represented a way to reintegrate themselves into society after a breakdown.

Personal crisis is often the precipitating factor in the messianic calling. A classic example of the calling through trauma is the story of Hung Hsiu-ch'uan, the messianic leader of China's Taiping Rebellion. Hung's messianic calling came after repeated failures to pass the civil service exam, failures that, in his society, had disastrous ramifications for himself and his family. After his third failed attempt, Hung had a breakdown. While ill and delirious, he had a vision of heaven in which an old man and a middle-aged man ordered him to kill the demons on earth. Hung recovered and tried once again to pass the civil service exam. After this failure, his cousin gave him some Christian tracts to read. These provided Hung with an understanding of his earlier vision and of his repeated failure to become a civil servant. He decided that the old man in his vision was God, the middle-aged man was Jesus Christ, and he was the Second Son of God, charged with the holy mission of saving the world from the evil destroying it. Soon afterward, Hung organized the God Worshipers Society, which, within a short time, was transformed into the Taiping army to challenge the Manchu dynasty.

The story of L. Ron Hubbard's calling to found the Church of Scientology is a present-day parallel to the story of Hung Hsiu-ch'uan. The son of a naval commander, Hubbard tried unsuccessfully to follow in his father's footsteps. He was a poor student, however, dropping out of one high school to be enrolled in another for "slow" and difficult students. His subsequent naval career was also checkered. Relieved of one command after an investigation, he was removed from duty altogether and admitted to the Oak Knoll Military Hospital after he reported sabotage that an investigation failed to substantiate. In 1945, two years after his release from Oak Knoll, in a letter to the Veterans Administration, Hubbard complained of mental difficulties and of long "periods of moroseness and suicidal inclinations" and requested psychiatric treatment.[2] He later maintained that it was during his hospital stay that he first received a message from God, which prompted him to found Scientology.

Usually, the first reaction to the call is resistance. To establish his credentials the messiah must officially demonstrate that he or she does not eagerly embrace such an exalted burden but only accepts it upon realization that there is no other choice. In social terms, it is not surprising that messianic etiquette dictates an initial resistance to the call.

The image that characterizes recruitment is surrender; the messiah must sacrifice himself to God's Will. In fact, the call, though manifested as an affliction, is more like a seduction, which in proper romantic fashion is initially resisted but ultimately heeded. The metaphor of spiritual marriage is commonly used to describe the relationship between a messiah and his god, and this union is not restricted to partners of the opposite sex. Aimee Semple McPherson, the messianic evangelist of the 1920s, for example, referred to herself as Christ's Bride. To underline the point, she habitually dressed in white. In a similar spirit, St. Bernard wrote of Christ as his "soul's Bridegroom." Contemporary male messiahs more frequently conceive of themselves as being a Second Son or as fulfilling the prophesied Second Coming. Their mystical kinship is achieved through blood, not marriage. For them, the concept of spiritual marriage characterizes the relationship they hold with their followers, a relationship that is not always just metaphorical.

Not surprisingly, messianic cults have long been associated with sexual scandal. Divine's followers would "vibrate" themselves into states of sexual frenzy while declaring their love for Father, and Jim Jones required his followers to describe their sexual fantasies about Father. While many messianic groups outlaw sex, their leaders usually exempt themselves from this ruling. Divine slept with his Rosebuds, his inner circle of young women; Jim Jones forced male and female followers to have sex with him, publicly boasting of his prowess; and Chuck Diederich, founder of Synanon, desexualizes his followers by requiring the men to have vasectomies and the women to shave their heads.

Sexuality is implicit whenever the idea of Grace is associated with effacement of the personality, with "giving oneself up to the Lord." There is an underlying sexuality in the relationship between a messiah and his god, just as shamans are literally "possessed" or "mounted" by spirits, as is so often described. Thus, when messiahs begin to consider themselves god, they frequently demand sexual submission from their followers.

The relationships within messianic movements are like nesting dolls, each doll identical but built to a smaller scale. The conditions that foster the development of messianic movements at a societal level are analogous to the causes of the breakdown that precipitates the messiah's own calling. Just as the movement represents a restructuring of the existing social order, so too does the messiah's calling represent a solution to his affliction, legitimizing a new relationship or status in society. To complete the analogy, the relationship between a messiah and his god is mirrored in the relationship between a follower and the messiah.

For both messiah and followers, entrance into a messianic movement constitutes spiritual rebirth. The messiah is reborn as God's Second Son, his followers reborn as his children. The recruitment process that the messiah undergoes is repeated by his followers. They too are required to give themselves up to God (in the person of his stand-in, the messiah) and forced to renounce their pasts, worldly possessions, attachments, and ideas. Rebirth for followers, like that for the messiah, is preceded by breakdown. Conversion takes place after a symbolic death, for in the messianic context, breakdown is a public manifestation of being special, singled out. Breakdown is a sign of Grace.

With rebirth comes a sense of purpose and revitalization. The messiah, having overcome his "demons," forges a new and important identity for himself, shared by his followers. He is the Savior, destined to rescue the world from imminent destruction, and they are the Chosen People who will implement his mission.

The dangers intrinsic to messianic movements have to do with this exalted self-vision. By his own proclamation and his followers' acquiescence, the messiah is beyond the law. Almost inevitably, the granting of limitless power to one person to wield over others as a natural right leads to abuse. God's powers are awesome enough even when they are restricted to abstract, indirect control, but when Father appears in the flesh to enforce his rules, it is another matter.

Self-delusion is the occupational hazard of messiahs. Even those who at first do not believe all their own rhetoric usually succumb in time to the self-deification they have promoted. With self-deification comes rigidity. Success breeds a certain contempt and a certain ruthlessness. Father Divine, for example, whose business instincts kept him more firmly planted on the ground than most, nevertheless eventually began to believe in his own pronouncements. The turning point for Divine came at the conclusion of his trial when the judge unexpectedly dropped dead. Undoubtedly amazed, Divine also perhaps dimly believed himself in some way responsible. If nothing else, the judge's opportune death planted in him the seed of self-delusion; it was after that time that Divine threatened anyone who opposed him with a similar fate.

Jim Jones, who included miracle healings in his Sunday sermons—the removal of "cancers" from members of the audience—was impressed with their efficacy even though he had
artfully prearranged for decaying chicken organs to be produced at the right moment. He began to believe that notwithstanding his chicanery, he must indeed have the power to cure.
Aimee McPherson, another healer, set aside a "miracle" room
in her Los Angeles temple, filled with discarded crutches and
wheelchairs.

The autobiographical account of Quesalid, a Kwakiutl shaman, details the self-deluding process. Quesalid became a shaman as a way to expose the profession. He accurately described
his first lessons as a peculiar mixture of pantomime; the techniques for inducing fainting, nervous fits, and vomiting; ob-
stetrical information; and the use of "spies" to report on the
private conversations of people, especially concerning the ori-
gins and symptoms of their illnesses.[3] His apprenticeship confirming his suspicions, Quesalid might have been satisfied with
his muckraking had he not been asked to treat a sick person who
had dreamed that Quesalid would cure him. The cure undid
Quesalid's resolve—it was an overwhelming success. After that,
Quesalid continued curing, building a reputation as a formidable
shaman. At first he retained some measure of objectivity, rea-
soning that his cures were successful "because he [the sick per-
son] believed strongly in his dream about me." But soon his
objectivity clouded, and Quesalid began to feel "hesitant and
thinking about many things." By the end of his narrative,
Quesalid was no longer skeptical. He believed in his cures and
took pride in his accomplishments, having concluded that some
forms of shamanism were less false than others.

In miracle workers less skeptical than Quesalid and less
grounded in reality than a man like Father Divine, self-delusion
assumes truly ominous proportions. In them, power runs its full

course, magnifying all the insecurities and ambivalences that drove them to their profession in the first place.

Jim Jones is a case in point. He never unraveled the knot of love and anger that pervaded his childhood. He loved his mother, hated his father, despised women, emasculated men. His obsession with parental power, with death, and with sexuality ran like a connecting thread throughout his life. It was not mere power that corrupted Jim Jones. Power exacerbated the strains that had been there all along. It enabled Jones to impose his fantasy on others. "How do you feel," Jones asked his followers, "when you say you want Dad to die, so you can die or do your own thing?" The question, repeated endlessly, rhetorically, became the leitmotiv of Jonestown.

The more he isolated his commune from the rest of society, the more bizarre his delusions became: he identified with the killer protagonist in *The Day of the Jackal*, who, in Jones's reading, was on a mission to rid the world of an important "Fascist"; he was obsessed with the idea of political torture and believed the CIA was stalking him, waiting to invade Jonestown and torture its residents; and he projected onto the "Fascists" many of the things he himself inflicted on his "children"—he abused, tortured, and killed, before anyone else could do it to him.

Tapes Jones recorded of himself at Jonestown (for like Nixon, Jones recorded everything) reveal compassion one moment, rage at another. He rambles, cursing in turn the traitors, defectors, the "fascist scum" who surround him. There are no transitions in Jones's monologue; the shifts are instantaneous and self-generated, for the outside world no longer penetrates his inner vision. Though there are moments of clarity and of intelligence, they are the remnants of an earlier self.

The creation of a messianic society is a radical act. If the attempt succeeds, it brings tremendous power to the messiah—

power that would be overwhelming even to the most well-adjusted individual. The messiah is hardly that. The adulation he receives confirms his belief in his superiority over everyone else, his true difference from the rest of society. His overweening belief in himself is the stick he wields for beating off his own insecurities. The excess of it reveals its other terrified side. So for the messiah, success is precarious, too. It is not based on a balanced view of the world and his place in it, but is instead like an enormous, tottering cardhouse that grows more fragile as it expands.

4 ≡

WHO JOINS CULTS

Most cult members are young—in their late teens or early twenties—white, and middle-class. Approximately 60 percent have attended a few years of college, but only 20 percent have graduated. Much of the available research indicates that cult members tend to come from intact families. Interestingly, there are half again as many males in cults as there are females.

I talked at length to many people who had left cults about their reasons for joining and their experiences as members.* My conversations with active cult members, on the other hand, were limited in all ways. They were reluctant to talk with someone who might be a skeptic—or worse, an enemy to their group—and thus their responses were guarded, often sounding like memorized recitations.

---

* Accurate information about cult memberships is hard to come by. Most cults do not cooperate with scientific studies; the few that do generally provide researchers with preselected subjects. The circumstances under which many studies have been made have biased their results. Researchers, in consequence, have had to depend upon personal interviews for their information. These reports are also skewed in some ways. Mental-health professionals have usually obtained their data from people seeking help, while sociological researchers have depended on the information offered by cult volunteers. But despite the difficulties in obtaining objective information, both the personal interviews and studies that have been conducted point to a pattern from which one can draw reasoned conclusions.

The ex-members with whom I spoke showed no signs of grave psychological disturbances. The majority related specific reasons for their receptivity to cult involvement. The most prevalent were the usual problems of adolescence: separation from their families, personal setbacks, and alienation from a world that does not provide them with set roles and clear direction. Many also cited pressure from a friend, spouse, or lover who was a member of the cult they joined. Not a few said they were attracted by idealism and spiritual quest.

Tim O'Brien's account of his attraction to The Way was typical of the alienation that makes many receptive to cult involvement.

"When I lived at home, I never really had to question myself with my family. I was always their son or their brother and they loved me for that. The same with my good friends. We never really had to talk about anything. We were friends, friends for life, and that was the extent of it.

"In college, it seemed like I was always being questioned. The rest of the guys on the dorm floor were schmucks. One guy got drunk every night; another guy was a backstabber and everybody knew it. There were two sophomores: one was just into getting high, always partied out, and the other was a jock—really stupid—into a fraternity called Kappa Zoo, just like *Animal House*. And the two guys who lived next door were really preppy, just like my roommate. One was getting high, the other just drank. And then there were a couple of minorities and basically kids who got stepped on. I didn't enjoy getting stepped on and I knew I shouldn't be, but there was nothing I could do—I was isolated.

"One of the kids who got stepped on, when the second semester rolled around, he disappeared. He transferred—never said good-bye to anybody, just split. I could see why. He was a member of a fraternity, and the guy sometimes stuttered. I'm sure it was because of the fact that he questioned himself and had a problem with his self-confidence; and he was a nice guy.

"I went to his fraternity one time where they're supposed to be fraternity brothers. We went to buy some marijuana from one of his brothers, and this guy was a total asshole to him. I couldn't believe it. *I* felt like punching him, and he wasn't even being that way to me. But he didn't stand up for himself, he just got mad internally. So I could see why in the middle of the semester he just walked out, said the hell with it.

"I can't say I didn't meet good people as the year went on, but the experience was so bad I just couldn't recognize it. I couldn't, at that point, accept anybody for what they were. As the year went by I became more cynical and eventually began to stutter. It was really crazy. I'd never had any kind of speech problem before in my life—and there were points when I couldn't talk anymore. I got sincerely depressed, because I realized at certain times, like when I came home from vacation, it was the first time I noticed I no longer cared about my personal appearance, and that really sorta scared me.

"Needless to say, The Way was on campus, and they had the alternative to offer. They were the only people who were different. They were the only people who appeared to be standing up for what they believed in and doing what they wanted to and not needing to get drunk or high or anything to have a good time. They were different. They were the alternative."

If Tim O'Brien's disillusionment with life away from home made him receptive to The Way, Alison Peters's account touched on another typical kind of vulnerability. Alison had been out of Children of God for well over a year when I spoke with her. She was past the early stages of deconversion, had analyzed her motivations for joining, and was embarked on a new life.

"I had been living with someone for three years and had just left the relationship, was down and out, and I was scattered. I was very vulnerable, to say the least. I was twenty-one. Because of leaving the relationship, I had just moved into a city where I didn't have any friends, and I was in an apartment working, trying to get myself back together and going to school, when Ed called me. I had known him in high school and he was into the Children of God then, had given me a lot of literature to read, but I just hadn't been interested.

"I was in need of friends, and he called me and said he was in town for vacation and had heard about me and George breaking up and would like to come and say hello. I told him over the phone, 'Look, I'm really in need of friends, but I don't want to hear your doctrine.' I had been raised a Catholic till I was twelve, when my family left the church, and at the time all this happened, I was not into seeking religion. I didn't really care about Jesus or God or any of that.

"Ed came to visit, and in a matter of a three-hour discussion, that very first night, I experienced an altered state of consciousness, which, at the time, I understood, through Ed, to be the Kingdom of God. That night I did not decide to join the Children of God, but I said in my mind, if I don't do this, I'll never be able to live with myself. I knew this was the peace of mind, the ideal, the ultimate I'd been searching for all my life, the one everyone had talked about—the Eastern philosophies, the vegetarians. I knew that this was it, that if I didn't pursue it, I'd be searching for the rest of my life."

"There's no question in my mind about when I decided to join," David Wallace, an intern at a New York hospital, told me. "It was the first day after I finished the hardest and the worst semester I'd ever done in my life—that third semester of medical school. I just did awful that semester; I'd never ever done so bad in my life. And it wasn't as though I didn't study, and I didn't think I was that unhappy. But God, I just did terrible. I had to take refreshers in two courses. I mean, I'd never gotten a D in my life!"

David had fallen into medicine. Doctors in his family went back four or five generations. "I went into it because I didn't know what else to do. My mom said to me one day, sort of jesting, but in truth, 'Look it, I don't care what you do . . . just get your M.D. first.' But she meant it.

"The first two semesters of medical school I lived at home because they had extension campuses. There were small classes and I had a wonderful time. So after being cozy my first year—doing well and learning a lot and having the benefits of home and all—and then being in an apartment for the first time after being in a dorm all my life, there was a lot of change. My two roommates were very aggressive scholastically, and I just couldn't cut it. Everything I did was wrong!

"After we finished the finals, I began thinking of the Divine Light Mission. I had heard of DLM in 1975, and all through 1977 the thought was there that there was this meditation I can always go to. As soon as I got the meditation in March, I felt like I was in like Flynn. No more problems."

Cult followers generally fall into several descriptive categories. The first is composed of essentially normal people who turn to cults at a moment of particular difficulty in their lives. A sudden loss, disappointment, or frustration of important expectations is the usual cause of the identity crisis that leads to cult conversion. The majority of today's cult followers probably fall into this category. Margaret Thaler Singer, a California-based psychologist who has counseled hundreds of cult members, estimates that 75 percent are basically "normal." Galen Kelly, a licensed investigator who became involved in the deprogramming business in 1975, agrees with her findings. His firm conducted a study based on one hundred "rehabilitation" cases they had handled over a period of four years. Most of those studied had been members of the Unification Church. Their results corroborated Singer's. G. Kelly Associates found that 68 percent were "stable" individuals who were experiencing "mild adolescent difficulties" at the time of their conversion.

Boston psychiatrist Dr. John Clark, on the other hand, maintains that, based on personal examination of people in all stages of cult involvement, about 60 percent are chronically disturbed and only 40 percent are essentially normal. The latter were susceptible to conversion either because of normal, though painful, "crises of maturation," or because they could not withstand the pressure exerted on them by an aggressive proselytizer.

The second category of cult followers is made up of people who have shown considerable evidence of developmental and emotional problems over an extended period of time. They have been described as "searchers" or "seekers," people looking for something, some magic belief or affiliation to fill up their lives. Unlike the first category of cult followers, whose sense of self is only temporarily impaired, these people have a poor sense of identity, which is bolstered by, as Dr. Clark puts it, "becoming another person in as many ways as possible." [1]

A final category is composed of disturbed people. According to all estimates, these are a minority among cult members. Some evidence suggests that truly psychotic individuals do not make good converts—that despite their initial enthusiasm for conversion and their comfortable acquiescence to the requirement to shut out the outside world, these people cannot easily maintain conversion. Sooner or later they experience a crisis and revert to their own personal version of reality.

There is also support for the truism that society's misfits are the classic cult followers. Many psychiatrists, sociologists, and anthropologists have long held that cult membership allows sociopathic personalities to legitimize deviant behavior; that cults or subgroups featuring possession states are the refuge for the mentally deranged, and that becoming "possessed" enables individuals to act out behavior not permitted in ordinary society. It is possible that this category of cult members is responsible for the sadistic practices of cults.

The anthropologist I. M. Lewis, however, has analyzed the membership of cults of possession throughout the world, and concurs with the predominant findings on American cults:* the number of genuine schizophrenics and psychotics is "small compared with the mass of ordinary 'normally' neurotic people who found some relief from anxiety and some resolution of everyday conflicts and problems in such religious activity." [3]

The decision to join a cult is determined by a number of interrelated factors, which account for a special vulnerability to cult proselytizing. These factors include cultural disillusionment and dissatisfaction in everyday life, both of which may be temporary features, having as much to do with the surrounding environment as with the personalities of converts. The other "vulnerability factors" are more directly related to family background and personal upbringing. The tendency to conceptual-

---

* In this context, the findings of a Louis Harris poll about the extent of "mental illness" in this country are cogent. According to the poll, one-third of American adults have had emotional problems at one time or another that affected their health. Twenty million have suffered prolonged mental problems. On the average, 10 percent of the general population is mentally ill, and in large urban areas, the incidence of serious emotional problems is as high as 23 percent.[2]

ize problems in a religious framework and a low tolerance for ambiguity are often personality characteristics of cult members. Dependency, the need to receive approval from others, and a susceptibility to trance states are the final determinants that create vulnerability to cult involvement.[4]

The informal testimonies of ex-cult members also provide a picture of cult membership. David Wallace characterized his fellow members of Divine Light Mission in this way: "There were all kinds in the cult. The people I ended up cavorting with were very intelligent and very idealistic people. But there were some real zonkers in the group, at least in New York. There were some wackos who should have been locked up a long time ago. You've got the fringe element there. I'd say, generally though, most people I knew seemed pretty normal and had a lot of potential. They were artists and people who dropped out of their first and second year of college. They were the most intelligent group, who maybe were not so career minded but definitely had heads on their shoulders. Maybe at the point they got in, they really didn't have their goals set—they weren't locked into a career. And even the people who were professionals usually had already been in the profession for three or four years and had bored out of it. But I'll tell you something interesting— most people got in because they knew someone who was already in. They did not see a sign."

Cult members' initial contact with the groups they join comes in two ways: through an acquaintance who is a member, as David Wallace indicates, or through aggressive proselytizing by members.

Robert Perez, with whom I spoke at length, joined Christ Brotherhood, a small cult run by an ex-professor of philosophy, because he fell in love with a member of the group and followed her in. Yet his underlying motivation was idealism. Far more than Tim O'Brien, Alison Peters, or David Wallace, who joined cults at moments of particular difficulty in their lives, Robert Perez was disillusioned with American society and looking for something better.

"You know I was born into a time when things were in complete chaos. Everything was breaking down and changing, and I was breaking down and changing, too. I went right along with it. I was caught up in certain currents in terms of drugs and politics and alternative life-styles.

"We read too much. We read too many books, and we believed what they said. We read the Bible. We read all the great antiwar novels. Our parents never read them. I read them and I believed it. Martin Luther King, Mahatma Gandhi, the whole thing—I believed it. Brotherhood. I just couldn't relate to the fact that people have to shoot one another, or to nationalism and wars and racial tensions. It seemed silly. Why do I have to shoot this guy? Why do I have to think of myself in competition with this fellow or that fellow? That I couldn't handle. I'd rather share."

Jane Kaufman, the member of Christ Brotherhood with whom Robert was in love, also articulated the sensibilities of the sixties. Graduated from college in 1969, she had spent a year in Europe and then moved as far away from her parents' home as possible, to the Pacific Northwest.

"In 1971," she said, "I settled in Oregon, where I worked in a natural foods restaurant and wrote in a women's paper. It was a marvelous time. Oregon was a hubbub of activity, communal things, spiritual questing. I was in a political orientation when I met these people, friends of Patterson Brown [the ex-philosophy professor] who really struck me. They'd been traveling around Mexico without any money, and they seemed very solid, very together. I thought these people were interesting, and this whole spiritual quest was hanging over me. I grew up in a family that never talked about God—a Jewish household with hardly any real religious orientation. I was very interested in what it all meant. And though it wasn't until three years later that I moved in with the cult, I was really ripe. Not so much because I was confused, but because I was searching."

Both Jane and Robert were impressed by the altruism of Christ Brotherhood. The group took in derelicts, pooled their food stamps, and tried to live as the true disciples of Christ. "You know," Robert explained, "if you get someone who's searching for that right way to live, not like the way people live in society—no classism, no racism, no this side of town and that side of town—but as brothers and sisters; if you take in drunks and speak righteously to the powers that be as well as to the man on the street, it's very powerful."

The atmosphere of idealism and alienation of the late sixties played a part in both Jane's and Robert's attraction to Christ Brotherhood, yet motivation was also very personal. For them, as well as for others, political rebellion spilled over into adolescent rebellion. The need to escape one's family and to reject the values it symbolized propelled many young people into cults.

Dr. Hardat A. S. Sukhdeo, a psychiatrist who has worked with many ex-cult members, believes that their families share common characteristics: "They are usually small, inward-looking, and centered around the nuclear family. They often contain a relatively passive father and a relatively domineering mother. The parents are often children of first or second generation immigrants." Like many first-generation Americans, they were torn between the values of their own parents and the desire to belong, to be a "real" American. In consequence, Dr. Sukhdeo asserts, "many paid the price that a conflict of values often exacts: a disinclination to trust their own feelings, a reluctance to show or even feel strong emotions." These parents lived for their children, working to win for them the material comforts, education, and financial security they had not had themselves. Dr. Sukhdeo suspects moreover that this pattern is predominantly Jewish, which in part accounts for his observation that a disproportionately large number of Jews join cults.*

Rebellion against one's family, Jewish or not, is certainly a prime motivation for joining a cult. In the classic analysis of Chinese brainwashing, "Communist Interrogation and Indoctrination of 'Enemies of the State,'" published in 1956, Drs. Lawrence E. Hinkle, Jr., and Harold G. Wolff list the characteristics of people most vulnerable to brainwashing. Rebellion against parents "and the way of life of the segment of society to which their parents belonged, including many of its standards, beliefs, and practices," figures prominently. According to Hinkle and Wolff, marginality and idealism are also important factors in successful brainwashing. The best subjects for brainwashing "were people who had few friends within their homeland, and no place, organization, or occupation there with which they were firmly identified." [5] They also felt a great sympathy with the "underdogs" of the world, with people who were "exploited" or "oppressed."

Many of these same characteristics are found in today's cult members: "Why did I join?" Jane Kaufman reflected. "I just know that I was trying to deal with a very strong conflict with my mother, and I had an incredible conflict with her . . . still do. She's kind of got everyone orbiting around her, all her kids and her husband. And I had to get away from her. I was very rebellious, stubborn, and also very adventurous. I was interested in doing it differently, and I wanted to do it. I didn't have many fears."

---

* Galen Kelly notes that in his experience the majority of cult members are Jewish, followed by Catholics and then Protestants.

Robert answered the question in this way: "I fell in love with Jane and followed her back there [to Christ Brotherhood]. I had been living in Los Angeles, working at a place called the Catholic Worker, which is a group of lay Catholics who have free soup kitchens and houses of hospitality on Skid Row and areas like that.

"I think my main motivation was alienation, alienation that was fueled also by a really strong desire to belong. If you don't have any desire to belong to something—ideals about families and closeness—you don't bother."

Robert's childhood had been difficult, his mother and siblings dominated by an erratic and tempestuous father. "My background was what they used to call a 'racially mixed' marriage. My father was Mexican, my mother a small-town Indiana girl. They met in the army, had a lot of babies. My father was an alcoholic, left the family, then came back. There was constant turmoil in our family. My father was a very intense person to live around, very temperamental and very demanding. He was always at somebody, and by the time I was a teenager, I was tired of it. And I was involved in the same situation at the Catholic Worker. People were having difficulties with one another, and everyone would sit down and have it out: 'I don't like the way you do this or do that' and on and on. In Christ Brotherhood, everyone was living together as brothers and sisters with the perfect father figure. Nobody argued with him. Everyone was just glad to do what he said. So I found peace, so to speak."

A major attraction of a cult is that it is structured as a family. New members are the "babes," older members their respected siblings. The leader is the spiritual Father and his wife, if he has one, the spiritual Mother. Impelled by feelings of loneliness, converts find immediate refuge in the welcoming bosom of the cult. "I felt like a child again in a lot of ways," Alison said. "I felt I had this void, that I was sick and needed to be taken care of and needed to be protected."

Cults provide a sense of community. Members are never alone: they live together, work together, share a common goal and purpose. They are spared the shock of loneliness that comes from growing up. Instead of leaving one's family, friends, and hometown for an indifferent and not terribly idealistic world, they simply replace it, at one fell swoop. Contrary to popular assumptions, a large proportion of cult members come from closely knit families. Leaving home for these people is especially difficult. While joining a cult involves a radical separation from their families, it does offer a substitute that is similarly engulfing. In fact, cult life often replicates the psychological patterns first established within the "real" family. Jane Kaufman, for example, formed a relationship with Patterson Brown that resembled that with her mother. She respected Brown's intellect and perceptions, felt in fact that he had the key to reforming her personality, yet she was never able to submit herself to him. She held out, and it infuriated him. With Brown, as with her dominant mother, Jane was engaged in a struggle for control. She was passively antagonistic, yet the struggle itself forged a bond between the participants. Never articulated, it was constantly acted out.

A strong argument can be made that cults represent an especially turbulent form of adolescent rebellion. Joining a cult is a way of breaking the ties to the home. Even the onus of responsibility for rejecting one's parents is removed, for the surgery is prescribed by the group and is carefully supervised by cult leaders.

"They told me that my problem was my mother and that I had to renounce her," Jane stated simply. "Whenever she would come around, I'd get into trouble. Patterson would just ignore her, and I rationalized it that he really saw through her and where she was at. When I got pregnant, Patterson's girl friend coached me about how I should handle the situation with my parents: not to tell them I was pregnant—and I didn't for a long time—and then to write them a really scathing letter about why I hadn't told them and how they could not act like grandparents and couldn't see this child and not to bug me."

Joining a cult is a form of rebellion that does not fail to elicit a strong response, with parents threatening court action, mental hospitals, and kidnapping. Equally important, though, is that joining a cult is a movement toward something familiar—to something that already exists within the convert.

"After I joined," Robert explained, "I used to tell my mother, when she would raise doubts about my involvement, when she'd notice changes in me she couldn't understand, 'It's everything you ever taught me, what I'm doing now. The groundwork was laid when I was just a child and you'd tell me about Dad's alcoholism, what the problems were, and how I should respond—be forgiving and be loving and not judgmental. Be a good person and don't do other people wrong.' "

Robert's gentleness and passivity were great attributes in Christ Brotherhood, where he was held up as a sterling example to more wayward members, Jane among them. He was acting out the part his mother had played in his family and that she had recommended to her son. "In my eyes, my mother was a very saintly woman who put up with a lot in her life. And she was a Catholic and couldn't do the sensible thing, which was to divorce this guy who was giving her such a hard time and to try and make a new life for herself, which is what she should have done. She'd pray on her rosaries, and every little gift was a gift from God."

"Taking the last place"—being humble, caring for drunks and

derelicts—Robert found a cult that reenacted the family trauma of his childhood. But despite his wishes, Christ Brotherhood was not a peaceful family, and Patterson Brown was hardly a perfect father figure—except, perhaps to Robert, whose own father was similarly temperamental, abusive, erratic, and violent.

For many young people, the war and cultural revolution were short-lived—romantic images of a decade larger than life. But while some felt cheated by time, left out of the great social movements that had divided the country, others were frightened by the extravagances that decade had released. They longed for rules, for segregated dormitories and all the other symbols of a watched-over world. The half-grown and timid were terrified by the new freedoms. It was as though the experiment had overrun the laboratory, and many of the scientists rushed for cover.

College students were not alone. The gravitation of the young toward stability or the semblance of stability was a phenomenon paralleled in the rest of the nation. Jimmy Carter's down-home values got him elected in 1976; Anita Bryant's crusade against homosexuality and the Right to Life movement were related phenomena, reactions to changes that, for the most part, had already taken place but that could not be comfortably faced or comprehended. Political introversion and self-absorption were a reaction to the decade's turmoil.

Cults were one expression of this theme, offering happiness and inner peace to all takers. But while the cults of the late sixties were a direct response to the war in Vietnam—a "galloping Orientalism" that symbolically embraced the cultures most antipathetic to American values—the subsequent cults represented a special hybrid that transformed the passivity, spiritual hunger, and desire for order into a profitable business form specializing in quick capital and the exploitation of labor. Members of these later cults received transcendent experiences rather than commissions for street hustling that rivaled the door-to-door activities of Fuller Brush salesmen in dedication and success. But unlike the Fuller sales force, cult members were not fired if they did not fulfill the daily quota. Failure was attributed to a deficiency in moral worthiness; conversely, the more you raised, the closer you were to God.

For saving the world from Satan entailed first and foremost salesmanship. Middle-class kids, whose parents complained they had never done an honest day's work in their lives, put in grueling eighteen-hour days without a murmur. Their parents were perplexed. Yet their motivation was obvious. The new cults were providing what cults had always provided and what parents, schools, and traditional social institutions had stopped providing—structure, purpose, routine, and order.

Moreover, cults offered drama. Members were told that their lives had a very real and very important significance: they had been chosen to save the world, to bear witness to Armageddon, to survive the holocaust of their fathers. In fact, the drama of life in the cults is one of their most important attractions. Ordinary existence is exalted and intensified, drab routine magically turned into spectacular Technicolor. In a brilliant review of *Mein Kampf*, written in 1940, George Orwell incidentally puts his finger on one of the primary attractions of messianic cults. Hitler, he writes:

> has grasped the falsity of the hedonistic attitude toward life. Nearly all western thought since the last war, certainly all "progressive" thought, has assumed tacitly that human beings desire nothing beyond ease, security and avoidance of pain. In such a view

of life there is no room, for instance, for patriotism and the military virtues. Hitler knows that human beings don't only want comfort, safety, short working-hours, hygiene, birth-control and, in general, common sense; they also, at least intermittently, want struggle and self-sacrifice, not to mention drums, flags and loyalty parades. Whereas Socialism and even capitalism have said to people "I offer you a good time," Hitler has said to them "I offer you struggle, danger and death," and as a result a whole nation flings itself at his feet.

"An important part of coming to the conclusion that you want to live with the cult," Robert Perez observed, "is the recognition of the impending nature of the apocalypse. They're very big on that. Their sense of reality is that the apocalypse is just around the corner. You know no one thinks of nuclear war as just one bomb here and one bomb there. It's like, puff—total event. It's not just the possibility of being drafted and going into the trenches, but total annihilation of the human race. And they hold out that if you live with them, you won't die."

Jane Kaufman: "The desire to be unique and special and maybe a little better than anyone else is what attracted me. . . . I felt, too, that there was a lot wrong with my personality that I wanted to change, and I thought that Patterson really had the key."

Alison Peters's motivation was a little different: "At the beginning when I got in, I had this feeling, I just want to be led, I just want to be told what to do. It's all too much for me to handle." She willingly accepted the stringent routine of the cult, accepted the discomforts of group living, although previously she had highly valued her privacy, and she even accepted the cult's determination that she marry the district leader, a man she barely knew. "I'd seen him about three times," she told me. "We took a few walks and read the Bible together and memorized our verses together. And that was really the extent of the relationship." Liking her fiancé, feeling attracted to him, were issues that didn't enter Alison's mind. What mattered was that she had been told that the marriage was the Will of God. The decision had been made for her.

David Wallace described the moment of joining the cult as a "release; dumping your wares right there and saying, 'Here I am.' " Committing himself to the cult liberated David from his characteristic perfectionism and ambivalence. "I always wanted to be more of whatever it was that I was doing. No matter what I did, I did well, but I never thought I was excellent. Like when I played tennis, I got national ranking, but I felt it's either continue or don't, and I'd cut it short because I didn't have the gumption to keep going. I felt I was missing out of accomplishing."

Joining the cult allowed David to stop being so hard on himself. "I told myself, 'Look, you're never going to be the best at your job. There are always people who will be better than you—always. With your family, you know you're never going to have a conversation with them, so what's the big deal? You know you're not going to be the best, so why sit there and fool yourself?' I remember saying to myself, 'Look, the only thing you have is this. The only thing you have that you can accomplish in this world is Divine Light Meditation with the Guru.' "

At first, entering a cult provides relief from the problems of ordinary life. Describing the appeal of Father Divine some fifty years earlier, Reverend Eugene Callender summed up the attraction of cult life: "Father Divine relieved his followers of any sense of responsibility for their lives. The only other place where I've seen that working is in prison. I was chaplain at Rikers Island. It was absolutely incredible. The guys there were happy. They were kidding around with each other and joking. They didn't like being locked up, but their behavior demonstrated the fact that they were happy. The guards told them when to get up, they had their food ready for them, they had clothes waiting for them, they had a work assignment to do, they were told when to go to bed, they had their recreation— their whole lives were managed by someone else. That's what Father Divine did. When they were released they went to pieces. When you got into the Kingdom, you were told who to sleep with, you were told what you had to do, you had no decisions to make for yourself, you ate well, and you lived comfortably. As long as you stayed in the Kingdom, you were happy."

Live-in cults in particular are rigidly planned, with every minute programmed so that the whole problematic issue of choice is eliminated. If any free time exists, converts are usually too exhausted to make use of it. There is literally no time to think, no time to assess alternatives, and no decisions to be made. New converts are admonished not to ask questions but simply to obey: " 'If you think, think, think / You'll stink, stink, stink / And you'll sink, sink, sink.' They taught us that because they didn't approve of thinking," Alison reported. "They said it got in the way of being close to God. I used to even ask the leaders permission to get a drink of water . . . but it felt very comfortable."

For David Wallace, learning not to question was not so comfortable. "Every time there was something you didn't understand, they'd tell you to 'stick it in your back pocket.' It was like you had all these extra notes on your desk, and eventually, one by one, you stuck them in your back pocket. I knew that one by one I was accepting things, and I didn't fight it. I just rationalized everything away. Everything was 'Grace.' Everything was because it was supposed to be.

"Being told just to accept was in some ways a relief—you can give up that constant struggle. And since it was rationalized as being of a higher spiritual order, the difficulty involved in accepting it makes it seem like it must be a good thing."

In fact, cult converts are told that the act of relinquishing responsibility is the first step in acquiring spiritual power. Giving up personal control to God (or the Master) allows the individual to symbolically participate in his Will and thus share his power. Thus, cults give you access to special power. Members feel different, special, singled out, and personally attended by God. They also feel superior to those outside the cult, privy to secret knowledge and secret power.

If the first lesson in power entails yielding all claims to it, the second lesson occurs during proselytizing. "Witnessing" teaches converts how to influence others, and though cults usually use biblical terms to describe the techniques, they do not neglect the salient points of salesmanship. In fact, the two prominent icons at the Unification Church's seminary at Barrytown, New York, are Reverend Moon and Dale Carnegie.

"At home," David Wallace remarked, "it was like all chiefs and no Indians. You know, I'm no dumber than anyone else there, but I just sit and feel like an outsider. But when you're out there giving the spiel witnessing, even when you're trying to be humble, there was a certain sense of power—of being listened to. I knew I could sway my audience. You become rich in your humility."

Intense daily prayer sessions also confirm converts' belief in their own special powers. Emotional release in this form is interpreted as spirituality. Visions, prophecies, and talking in tongues are believed to be direct communiqués from God, tangible proof of one's special status. These moments of "heightened experience" are the explicit rewards for all the hard work and self-sacrifice. According to David, Divine Light Mission instills in members that "the purpose of human life is to have Darshan with the Living God," Darshan being the sacred ritual in which cult members kiss the Guru's feet. "When I did it," David told me, "I was really high. Even though I've never taken Quaaludes, it was the way people have described that. Like walking through water. Everything was completely slowed down. Like when I've done grass, everything stopped. Sounds just reverberated, everything was in slow motion. Most people snap. Some see light—some leave their bodies. It is a very powerful time, and believe me, a couple of those experiences can keep you going for years!"

Many of today's cults combine traditional values—hard work and Good Works—with a spirituality that resembles nothing so much as a drug trip. Though historically cults have often incorporated ecstatic experience, the particular version of ecstasy available in contemporary cults derives as much from the American counterculture as it does from traditional Christian mysticism.

The paramount place of ecstasy in today's cults may be, in part, simply another manifestation of a widespread general self-absorption in this country, cult members having discovered that self-denial can be as engrossing as self-indulgence. Historically, though, trance states and altered forms of consciousness are usually practiced by groups denied access to conventional forms of power, mystical power becoming a substitute for political and social power. Despite the fact that it is the members of privileged classes who are presently adopting these forms of self-expression, impotence—or perceived impotence—is undoubtedly an element in their motivation.

In objective terms, the power that cult members "possess" is largely illusory. It is not based on an externally validated authority. Even the power experienced in witnessing is indirect. The role of the cult member is, after all, that of a salesperson. Most, in fact, admit that they dislike witnessing, that it is a humiliating experience they endure as a moral test. And while rising to a difficult challenge certainly creates a sense of power, it is hardly the power of a person who commands undisputed authority. Rather, it is an example of what the writer Elizabeth Janeway has characterized as "the power of the weak." As David Wallace put it, "in the cult you get up so you can get down again."

When we ask ourselves who joins cults, it is important to remember that cults are not alien to the culture, but part of it. They reflect and refract it, incorporating the same values and trends as well as creating new values and trends. Cults are not only cultural hybrids, however, but emotional hybrids that combine adolescent rebellion with childlike dependency. Contrary to our prejudices, most cult followers are not outcasts or freaks, but ordinary people who face the problems and insecurities endemic to the species. The notion that only "crazies" join cults is misleading. What we are really trying to assert with that assumption is that it can't happen here, it can't happen to you or me. Whether we like it or not, the facts speak otherwise.

5

THE FIRST STEPS
OF INDOCTRINATION

Conversion is predicated on stress. Mass conversions generally occur not only during periods of social upheaval,
when people naturally gravitate toward simplistic ideologies and
messianic movements, but also when people are deliberately
placed under stress. The latter—aggressive conversion—simu-
lates the disorientation that occurs naturally in times of social
crisis by exacerbating fear, conflict, and guilt within its subjects.
Its techniques are designed to break down preexisting beliefs
and loyalties and replace them with new values and commit-
ments. These techniques are found in a variety of contexts: in
traditional rites of passage, religious orders, prisons, the armed
services, some political movements, and religious cults.

There are, however, crucial differences among these contexts
in their use of aggressive conversion techniques. In some, participants are informed about the process and undergo it
willingly; in others, informed consent does not exist. The
amount of time participants are subjected to these techniques
also varies. In traditional rites of passage, for example, conversion techniques are employed for a clearly delimited period of
time as preparation for entry into a new social status, while in

cults like the Unification Church, they are incorporated as a permanent aspect of everyday life. It is also important to distinguish the various circumstances under which conversion takes place: when, where, how, under whose auspices, and to what purpose.

In all conversions, however, the general process is similar. It occurs in three stages. First the individual is isolated from his past life, cut off from his former position and occupation as well as from those with whom he has emotional ties. Isolation is physical—separation from home, family, and place of work—as well as symbolic. It is common practice for the novitiate to be stripped of his name and his tangible belongings, thus symbolically being stripped of his former identity. In prisons, inmates are given numbers for identification; in rites of passage, all novices are referred to by the same generic name; in religious orders and some cults, members are rechristened with new names.

In the second phase of conversion, the loss of name and identity is reinforced by inducing the novice, emotionally and intellectually, to surrender his past life. Humiliation and guilt are the basic tools in the psychological dismembering of the former self.

In the third phase, the convert assumes a new identity and a new world view. The rehabilitated criminal, the born-again Christian, and the African girl who has just undergone her tribe's puberty ritual all reflect the assumption of new identities. Appropriately, the symbols of death and rebirth pervade the conversion process, for indeed, social death and rebirth are what conversion is all about.

The appeal of cults in America today is in part a natural outgrowth of the changes this society has recently undergone. But some groups have arisen that deliberately exploit the vulnerabilities of people in crisis. Aggressive conversion, or "brainwashing" as its extreme version is often called, has been used as a means to convert unsuspecting subjects and to maintain their conversion. The Unification Church, for example, calls itself dozens of different recruiting names, so new converts frequently don't know that they are joining Reverend Moon's church. Similarly, The Way International attracts people through performances of its rock bands, which do not make their affiliation known. While groups like Scientology or Lifespring may identify themselves from the outset, they do not inform the potential convert about the total nature of the commitment they are soliciting. Given only partial information and then subjected to intensive indoctrination, the newcomer may no longer be capable of freely deciding whether or not he wishes to stay by the time he knows all the facts about a group. Much of this chapter will be devoted to describing the first stages in this form of indoctrination.

The very first step in the indoctrination process is to attract the attention of the potential convert. Proselytizers must be able to spot likely targets and to engage their interest. For many cults, university campuses and college towns offer the ideal setting. Their representatives look for people who seem lonely and footloose, or for transients, people carrying suitcases and knapsacks. Once he or she spots the mark, the proselytizer engages the person in conversation, trying to search out areas of interest and concern. Acceptance, friendship, and understanding are the initial bait. Within the space of a brief encounter, the proselytizer must manage to win the potential convert's trust and desire to continue the acquaintance. The Moonies have dubbed this procedure "love bombing."

Alison Peters, a former member of Children of God, recalled love bombing in shopping malls. She'd look for people who seemed, as she put it, "sheepy, people who looked lost and vulnerable." Once she'd found them, she'd follow the techniques outlined in the pamphlets that all members of Children of God were required to memorize. "You'd begin by picking on things that you felt were personally interesting to them, in order to gain their trust." While she was talking to them, she would stare fixedly into their eyes, the classic technique of hard sell. As she described it, "It was the whole thing of exuding confidence, of maintaining direct communication so forceful that you're always completely in control. In the pamphlet, they described it in biblical terms: you were supposed to 'Let the Holy Spirit work through you.' The eye-to-eye contact was called 'letting the Light of Jesus come through your eyes into the other person's eyes.'

"You'd look for the weak spots in people. When the person would bring up something that was uncomfortable for them, you'd use that as an example of how there's so much wrong with the world. Then you'd generalize about the particular problem. The generalizations were used to create a feeling of comfort, to make them feel that they're not alone and that you understand. Then the generalizations became specific. When it happened to me, for example, Ed used my relationship to George as an example of how so many people are going through divorces and breakups. Then he picked it apart and related it to other things I'd done in my past that were similar. You have to play up to the feeling that I had and all these people have, of having no meaning, no sense of real security, no sense of what was going to happen in the future, and the fear of just continuing to repeat old mistakes."

Lonely, confused, and besieged by self-doubt, Tim O'Brien was the perfect mark for cult proselytizers. Suddenly he found himself the object of determined attention. An upperclassman who lived in his dormitory began love bombing Tim. As Tim described it, "He began to follow me around, basically. He would always be there. There were points when I felt crowded in by him because I could never get away from him. He was like a punching bag that was weighted at the bottom. You knew you could do anything to him, push him away, step on his toes, tweak his nose—he was always there. You could not get rid of him."

While Tim was flattered by the attention and indeed welcomed the company, like so many others who experience cult courtship he was somewhat disoriented by its intensity. "There were times when I felt totally closed in and in a sense, losing my identity. In a way, spending time with Hugo scared me. It was sort of seeing what life would be like in The Way. It was total isolation from everything and everyone else. I guess it was just a withdrawal into this organization. It was scary in that sense, that I could see that you just couldn't get along with the other people. You didn't have the same beliefs." Loneliness, however, won out. Tim enjoyed the company of the other Way members and was glad to have a place to go on weekends and friends to be with. As the year progressed, he became more and more involved.

The love-bombing phase of the indoctrination process varies from cult to cult. The Way's approach, for example, is decidedly low-key. Students are not pressured to drop out of school and commit themselves full time to the cause. Their conversion evolves gradually, and hard-core indoctrination takes place only months after prolonged love bombing. Divine Light Mission is similarly structured. Former member David Wallace managed to complete medical school and internship while a member of the group. During all those years, he lived apart from the group, only visiting the ashram during his spare time.

Among other groups, however, indoctrination is highly structured and intense, reminiscent of the classic brainwashings that took place in China in the late forties and early fifties in the attempt to remold workers and political deviants to conform to party dictates.

In China, those slated for "reeducation" or "thought reform" were first removed from their homes and families to remote centers, where isolation was tantamount to imprisonment. There they were subjected to a program of hard physical labor, while at the same time they had to learn an enormous mass of ideological material. These dual requirements made relaxation, privacy, and objective reflection impossible, gradually producing a state of exhaustion in the trainees. The debilitating effect of unrelieved pressure was compounded by the institution of "study" groups to help trainees learn the new material. In essence these study groups were forced confessionals, where the high priests and acolytes of the new order pressured the convert to renounce his past life and accept a reformed identity. It usually took about six months to produce a breakdown in the trainee. By then, the combination of prolonged exhaustion, the tension of constant self-questioning and peer criticism, the pervasive atmosphere of uncertainty (poor students often just disappeared, giving rise to rumor and anxiety), and the sense of helplessness aggravated by unrelenting pressure would bring about an emotional collapse. Once the subject's resistance had been broken, the need for some sort of order predisposed him to accept new ideas.

The Chinese call the moment of collapse "tail cutting," for the trainee has finally cut his ties to the old society. It is at this moment that much of the new material, which has been absorbed only superficially until then, begins to take on real meaning.

Training, however, did not end upon graduation. Continued

participation in mandatory study groups served as an enduring moral censor against reversion to old ideas and values, maintaining the fear and tension essential to successful brainwashing. The apprehension about "wrong" thought became a permanent way of life. Many Chinese graduates of thought reform were terrified lest they talk in their sleep or reveal their doubts through a slip of the tongue.[1] Moreover, as ideology depended on the vagaries of power politics, it was constantly subject to unpredictable changes and modifications, creating a state of permanent insecurity in the individual.

Among today's cults, the indoctrination techniques of Reverend Moon's Unification Church closely resemble the Chinese example (though they are tempered by the democratic context in which the church operates). As Moon himself was imprisoned by the Chinese Communists, it is more than likely that he learned these techniques firsthand.

Like the Children of God and The Way, Moon's Unification Church uses "love" to attract the newcomer. Moon proselytizers working the street spot likely prospects and invite them to come to dinner or a lecture in their communal home. After this initial visit, where visitors are plied with food and attention, they are cajoled to join their new friends at a weekend retreat.

The retreat is an isolated camp that resembles an idyllic paradise where everyone loves and accepts everyone else at first sight. Christian ideals are really practiced. Members welcome guests as long-lost family. They watch over, care for, and in fact, never allow newcomers to be alone or out of sight of the proselytizers who first "hooked" them. Guests are accompanied to the bathroom and fall asleep within an arm's length of their personal Moonies, who watch their every move and report it to their colleagues.

Moonies refer to their group as a family and christen their guests with baby names. Indeed, potential converts are treated like indulged children: their hands are held, and they are plied with extra portions at meals, which often consist of "kiddie" food—milk, cereal, cookies, and ice cream.

It is difficult for visitors to resist their hosts. Guests are placed in an uncomfortable position: cut off from the outside and unable to communicate with anyone but Moonies (for guests are prevented from having private conversations with one another), they are outnumbered. The generosity of their hosts also militates against criticism or resistance.

Much of the immediate attraction of the group is the emotional experience of community among peers. From the moment of entry, the novice is never alone. All activities—cooking, exercises, lectures, eating, and sleeping—are done in a group. This family atmosphere is very appealing, especially to recent college graduates or dropouts faced with an alien adult world.

As is characteristic of brainwashing, in the Unification Church nutrition and sleep patterns are altered, promoting a state of exhaustion, which lowers intellectual and emotional resistance. In Chinese thought-reform centers, lectures (up to fifty-six hours per week) were interspersed with physical exercises and games (volleyball and baseball) and followed by group self-criticism sessions. Similarly, in the Unification Church the days are crammed with structured activity. Hard work is interspersed with games, singing, and lectures, so that each waking moment is occupied and there is no time for reflection. This pace serves to overwhelm the guest and condition him for conversion.

One ex-Moonie, Christopher Edwards, described the procedure as follows: "You were cajoled to give up control to a person for five minutes, and that person structured your environment for that time. Then you gave up control for another twenty minutes, following the wave of group singing. Then you listened to lectures giving up your critical control, since control in the discussion groups was contingent on accepting the ideology of the lectures." [2]

Lectures follow the emotional high pitch produced by group singing. They introduce the doctrine of the Unification Church and are purposefully repetitive, designed to habituate the listener, even the initially bored listener, to key phrases and ideas.

Lectures break up into "study groups," where the material is discussed. As in the Chinese "group cells," confirmed converts always outnumber newcomers. Far from being open discussions, these study groups serve as training sessions that condition guests to become emotionally dependent on their hosts.

In China, the purpose of such sessions was to ensure that everyone understood the lectures and accepted them unequivocally. Following the study groups were self-criticism sessions in which each person was prevailed upon to criticize his or her life using proper Communist behavior as a yardstick. Past and present faults were dissected by the group, whose members expressed their own zeal for reform in the intensity with which they tore down each other's defenses. Once a person demonstrated sufficient humility and offered a satisfactory confession, the group's attitude would soften and become more accepting. The very process of confessing, then, provided satisfaction. It rewarded confessors with a sense of belonging and acceptance that was particularly valued after having been reviled and rejected. Some people, especially those who had not previously had a clear commitment or goal, experienced this process as a rebirth. They were exhilarated by their feelings of "belonging" and "purpose." For these people Chinese brainwashing was like a religious conversion.

In the Unification Church as well, study groups exert peer pressure to elicit confessions.* Visitors are asked to tell their goals for the day and receive praise when these conform to the official doctrine. Those who confess self-doubts and insecurities are hugged and doubly praised. The message is clear: submissiveness gets love, recalcitrance doesn't. Manipulation of this sort is reinforced by games like Simon Says, which instill obedience in players and condition them to respond instantly to authority.

In short, love, at first given so unconditionally, becomes a reward to be earned through proper behavior. The criteria become increasingly stringent. The effort to try to learn the required response to gain approval, combined with a lack of sleep, inadequate nutrition, and constant, strenuous activity that allows no time for rest or reflection, begins to take a toll. The guests lose their critical faculties. Exhausted and emotionally overwrought, they find it easier to lie low, keep quiet, and not provoke the anger and disapproval of the group by asking questions and expressing doubts about the world view they are being asked to embrace. It is a relief to forget, to throw oneself into the waves of emotion that group prayer and singing excite. After a while, visitors hit the sleepwalking stage, moving automatically through activities without thinking. The disorientation and identity loss necessary for successful conversion have taken hold.

---

* It is the use of group pressure that primarily distinguishes the Chinese indoctrination techniques from the Russian interrogation methods from which they derive. The Russians elicited "confessions" (as in the purge trials of the 1930s) through the use of a single interrogator. Prisoners were subjected to long periods of isolation, broken only by interrogation sessions, which most prisoners came to anticipate as a welcome change. An intimacy often grew between the prisoner and his interrogator, who was so knowledgeable and involved in the details of the former's life history. The dependency that the prisoner developed on his interrogator became an important means of eliciting his confession and compliance.

Whether indoctrination takes place in a single weekend or over a period of months, the groups that practice aggressive conversion all follow similar patterns. *Est* weekends, for example, intersperse endless hours of lectures about the nature of life and existence with mental exercises ("processes") designed to eradicate old patterns of behavior and thought, and with grueling, often vitriolic personal encounters with the *est* trainer.

It is common for these groups to use intense emotionality to obscure the manipulative nature of their conversions. Tim O'Brien's description of The Way's meetings is reminiscent of the Moon weekends. "The fellowship meetings were a very high emotional time. You sing, you pray out loud, and it's very personal. They'd read from the Bible and then they'd have manifestations from God—speaking in tongues, prophecy, and all that. It was encouraged to speak what was on your mind. And you definitely felt a sense of security, of never being put down. I guess they also really laid the ground rules of what you could say and how you could act."

Alison Peters talked about the prayer sessions of Children of God in virtually the same way. "The prayer sessions were the best time. You'd walk away so high. There'd be visions and prophecies and speaking in tongues." These peaks masked her growing fear of the leaders. "I was very afraid of the leaders and wanted so much their approval, for the rewards. The rule was that the only way to get closer to God was to emulate and obey those who are closer to God than you, those who've passed the tests and trials God has put them through." Those who didn't follow the "rule" were called on the carpet for individual sessions during which they were psychologically abused by the group leaders.

The Moon weekend and similarly intensive programs provide, in miniature, all the chronological elements necessary for effective brainwashing: the stripping of identity, dissociation from the past, and the adoption of a new identity. The first stage capitalizes on personal vulnerability. Proselytizers seek out vulnerable people because their attention is easily captured. They are capable of listening to certain kinds of information with greater attention, with less humor, and with less ability to just throw it away than the ordinary person walking down the street.

The second phase of aggressive conversion involves inducing the individual to disconnect from his past. It involves breaking down the personality. Stress, as the Moon weekend illustrates, is the most crucial element in this phase of the process. Sufficient stress must be imposed without relief or time to recover, so that the individual is thrown off balance. He must begin to feel confused about himself and begin to question his basic assumptions.

This phase requires that the individual begin to float between two worlds, detached from his past and not yet connected to his future. This "betwixt and between" state has been described by anthropologists talking about rites of passage in traditional societies and dubbed the "liminal" stage. Rites of passage, like other forms of conversion, are designed to transform the individual. The rite orchestrates the transition into a new social status: in initiation rites, boys become men, and girls, women; in mourning rites, human beings are transformed into spirits; and in the rituals surrounding birth, the newborn become more than just living creatures, they become social beings. Before a new social status can be acquired, however, the previous one must be dropped. The novice must become nothing before he can become a new something; he must take off his old outfit before putting on the new. The naked moment, before the new clothes are on and the discarded ones are strewn about the floor, is the liminal period. It is a time of great danger and great potential. To achieve it, novices are deliberately disoriented, frightened by masked monsters, told terrifying stories, isolated in remote areas.

The second phase of indoctrination is analogous to the liminal state. The old personality must be destroyed before a new one can take its place. Some psychiatrists believe brainwashing must be understood primarily as a physiological process having to do with the way the brain handles information. As will be discussed in more detail in chapter 7, brainwashing alters the neurological patterns that determine behavior and constitute what we call personality. The modus operandi for this transformation is stress. The stress imposed in the brainwashing setup represents an avalanche of new information that cannot be easily or quickly integrated. Not only does it conflict with much of the old information the individual carries about, but there is simply too much of it to absorb. If you remove a subject from his ordinary setting, away from his previous information base, his culture, and do not allow him adequate time to integrate fully the new information, nor time to sleep and dream (an essential part of information consolidation and elimination), something radical occurs. The "fabric of the mind" rips, and a change takes place that can be compared to the emergency switching of a train onto a different track.[3]

The first instance of this shifting of the mind occurs early on in the conversion process. The trance state and related altered states of consciousness experienced as "spiritual revelation" can occur after only a few days or even a few hours. The ingredients are exhaustion, overstimulation, tension, and excitement. In itself, trance is not detrimental, nor does it produce radical, long-lasting change. If the individual is allowed to rest and sleep, the altered state will disappear and the person will return to normal. In fact, temporary ritualized, formalized dissociated states are common features of religions and cults and found worldwide.

What is unusual about many of our contemporary cults is that they do not allow the individual to return to normalcy, but rather attempt to maintain the dissociated state. The disruption of sleep patterns, the constant frenetic activity, the repetitive lectures and the emotional prayer/chanting sessions, in combination, are calculated to prevent the individual from returning to his familiar mental track.

Cult teachings reinforce the techniques that produce this altered state. Spirituality is presented as a goal diametrically opposed to rationality. Thinking is condemned as an obstacle to true spiritual being, and cult members are admonished and even punished for just looking as though they were engrossed in thought. They are encouraged and coerced to turn off their "material" minds. As Alison Peters expressed it, "The whole point in the cult was to stay in the Kingdom of God, which meant basically staying in the Spirit of God." The way to get into that "spirit" was through repetitive chanting, which constituted a form of self-hypnosis. "You kept on repeating, 'Thank you Jesus, thank you Lord. Praise you Lord, thank you Jesus.' It could be done out loud or it could be done internally. After a while I could snap into that state of mind after only a word, like 'Hallelujah' or 'Praise be.' I didn't need to go through the whole chanting."

Moonies also depend on chanting and prayer to keep converts in line. Even after conversion, any "free" time is spent in carefully monitored prayer sessions and group confessionals. These emotionally charged encounters help to keep doubts and other unacceptable thoughts at bay. The Unification Church has also developed its own form of meditation called "centering." As a former member described it, "Centering is centering yourself on Moon's definition of God. You're instructed to concentrate on the thinkings of the church at all times and take the upper hand in any threatening situation. You are to assume dominion over the people you're around, because you're the enlightened one." [4]

Banishing thought strips away another layer of the personality, another hunk of the individual's mode of operation developed in response to long-term interaction with the "real" world. The granting and withholding of approval comes to replace the complex evaluation system that serves as the basis for behavior and determines action. Subjects become more willing to act on command from an external authority and less able to act independently.

"Each time they'd ask me to do something more," David Wallace said of the Divine Light Mission, "I'd sort of swallow my pride and try it. Witnessing and soliciting are things I always felt queasy about. But you do it. You eventually lose your gut feelings. You're given directions and you follow them even though you know they're wrong. Like the special charitable projects, when you knew all the money was going for new toys for the Guru. You know it's wrong, but you do it anyway."

Prayer, chanting, and centering do not resolve conflict, but reduce or temporarily obscure it, without jeopardizing the supremacy of the group. Alison Peters depended on these techniques for getting through the ordeal of witnessing six days a week and for banishing any thoughts that conflicted with her new life. "I would just pray before doing anything. Say a prayer for ten seconds like 'Lord help me to get that soul' and get myself psyched up. It was almost like sticking the program card in. And then I'd close with some chanting to be sure that I'd really be high. It was the feeling that I'm here and talking to you and there's a purpose that I have in mind, but there would be no interfering thoughts about, let's say, what kind of reactions you may be having toward me. Doubting, questioning, checking myself out—none of those interjecting thoughts would come in."

The replacement of thought by emotion occurs at another level as well. Official cult doctrine translates into intellectual terms the emotional system of reward and punishment that constitutes the underpinning of cult life.* Fear and love, the natural correlates of dependence, are given a conceptual base in dogma. According to this dogma, the world is doomed: a powerful, wily Satan subverts all that is good and holy, invading unguarded souls and filling them with doubt and temptation. He lurks at every corner, awaits every careless moment, and then attacks, tempting the holy with the sins of the material world. His favorite target, naturally, is "heavenly children," and he redoubles his efforts to win them over. In the Unification Church as well as in other cults, sensual desires are considered sinful. Hunger, sleepiness, and sexual urges are all the iniquitous work of Satan. His legion of demon helpers perches on the eyelids of the faithful to make them fall asleep during lectures; they lounge all over the "children's" bodies when they are sleeping and must be brusquely shaken off in the morning. Even food must be consecrated to dispel any lingering contamination from Satan's world. Salvation is possible only through membership in the church, and membership entails renouncing everything and everyone else.

---

* This "translation" is also utilized in Communist indoctrination techniques. In fact, it has been observed that indoctrination is more successful in individuals who have a pre-existing emotional or intellectual framework that can be translated into Communist terms. Strong feelings of guilt associated with highly organized systems of moral values make for an especial vulnerability. Of the foreigners subjected to Chinese thought reform, those who are devoutly religious, with a profound sense of sin, make the most promising candidates.[5]

By attributing to Satan desires and thoughts that the rest of society considers natural and human, cults place their members in an unending emotional and intellectual bind. Told that Satan is ubiquitous, the cult member is constantly reminded of that truth through his own experience. He is forced to reject all "selfish" feelings within himself, and thus when they inevitably intrude—when the convert becomes sleepy, hungry, thoughtful, or sexually aroused—he believes that Satan is trying to possess him. Even his ability to question the dogma becomes emotionally charged, because the very act of questioning has been defined as evil. The constant tension of having to reject innate aspects of oneself is exhausting. The convert's own humanness places his membership in the group and his "salvation" in jeopardy.

David Wallace described the dilemma vis-à-vis the Divine Light Mission: "You see, in DLM, nothing you do has value unless it is related to the Guru and the Ultimate Purpose. So in the cult you're not allowed to rest. There isn't a level of acceptance where you can just be. Everything has this panoramic intonality to it. Everything's Ultimate. My God, if you take a shit, it's Ultimate. They actually tell you to sit there and meditate while you're on the john. And you feel tremendous guilt for not being able to be focused on the Ultimate all the time."

In time, the tension of continually fighting off Satan and remaining a dutiful child while undernourished and exhausted takes a toll. The symptoms are familiar. Chris Edwards describes his own experience: "I can't concentrate. I can't even read anything that challenges Father's words; it gives me headaches. I can't read a book or newspaper in depth anymore, it hurts my eyes and I fall asleep after several lines." His conversion has been a success.

6 ≡

BREAKING THE WILL

In 1933, a German journalist, Charlotte Beradt, began writing down the dreams of her compatriots under the Nazi regime.[1] She believed that these dreams revealed the process by which the totalitarian state insinuated itself into the German psyche. Moreover, dreams, unlike diaries and other conscious explanations and accounts, were relatively free from self-censorship, ingenuously articulating the conflicts faced by individuals in that society. Many of the dreams were transparent wish-fulfillment fantasies: Germans who in their waking lives opposed the regime would discover in sleep that Hitler was really not so formidable or terrible. In these dreams, the determination to resist would vanish almost magically: a man who dreamed that he was going to tell a joke forbidden by the Reich discovered in the telling that he had mysteriously altered the punch line, thus making the joke innocuous; a man who bravely decided to write a formal letter of protest to the Nazis found himself mailing a totally blank piece of paper; a woman made uncomfortable by the singing of the Horst Wessel song found she was less embarrassed if she joined in. Frequently, dreams anticipated the moral capitulation of the dreamer: a man who dreamed he went to the shoemaker to have new soles put on was told that only the SS were to have new soles; shortly afterward he joined up.

Cults in America

The dreams of the Third Reich record the environment of pressure and propaganda that eroded the individual will. How this occurred sheds light on the indoctrination practices of some cults. For the problem all indoctrinators face is maintaining conversion over time: How do you break the will of an individual and keep it broken? How do you ensure continued submission and obedience? The Third Reich provided many examples. Not only did it break the will and determination to resist of thousands of its subjects, but it also undermined the will to survive in those incarcerated in concentration camps.

One element in the "breaking" of the German population was disorientation. An atmosphere of uncertainty and fear was deliberately created so as to impress upon the average citizen that nothing was as it had been and that no one was safe any longer. Surprise was manipulated to this end: arrests took place in the middle of the night, rumors about concentration camps were circulated, and important members of society, in particular the once sacrosanct aristocracy, were abruptly denounced.* The effect of this policy, as the German theologian Paul Tillich described it, was the "feeling that our existence was being changed." It bred an atmosphere of permanent insecurity, which debilitated those subjected to it and thus allowed the Reich to flourish.

In part, the totalitarian state is sustained because individuals terrorize themselves—they become accomplices in their own tyrannization, censoring what they say and even what they allow themselves to think and feel. The dreams of the Third Reich reflected this internal process. People commonly dreamed that a familiar object would begin to talk, revealing all the private thoughts of the dreamer: lamps, favorite cushions, mirrors, and

---

* The attempt to suppress information about the camps occurred only after they had become, in 1941, "death" or extermination camps.

dutch ovens suddenly acquired voices with which to betray
their owners, repeating jokes about Goebbels's appearance and
Hitler's harangues. Every passing thought that did not totally
conform to the orthodoxy of the Reich was experienced as subversive: housewives dreaming of their garrulous ovens had come
to fear themselves.

In many of the contemporary cults a similar process of intim-
idation occurs. All aspects of behavior that the cult considers
unacceptable are classified as Satanic. As these categories include basic human functions, their denial creates a constant
strain. The struggle to rid the self of these urges becomes a
form of self-terrorization not unlike the attempt of Germans to
purge from themselves any independent thoughts.

The dread of being completely revealed is common to small
children who fear their parents can read their minds, as well as
to the subjects of totalitarian states and authoritarian cults. The
small child feels powerless in relation to his parents, as do adults
subjected to totalistic rule. Indeed there appears to be a natural
tendency to revert to childlike behavior under such conditions.*

The testimony of ex-cult members confirms this observation.
Many describe watching themselves and their "brothers" and
"sisters" gradually become incapable of making even the sim-
plest decision. Like children, they ask permission to go to sleep,
to have a drink of water, and to go to the bathroom. Chris
Edwards's sensation of shrinking in size after only a weekend at
a Moon retreat is explicit: "I found myself in front of the sink,"
he writes. "How curiously large it seemed. The bowl looked
immense, much too big for my little hands." In psychological

---

*As psychologist Bruno Bettelheim has observed, "as soon as a dictatorship arrogates to
itself the parental position, treats us all as incompetent children, and we let ourselves
be put in this position, this very fact makes us regress in our unconscious to the infantile stance." [2]

literature, the image of shrinking is considered a symbol of death, and indeed, much of what goes on in the indoctrination process has to do with killing the adult personality.

The Third Reich undermined the will of the German population through fear and disorientation and fostered a process of self-terrorization that weakened the integrity of individuals, bringing out unconscious dependencies and the tendency to regress. The dreams Charlotte Beradt recorded reflect the effort of people to purge from themselves any independent thoughts and inner convictions that might jeopardize survival.

What is remarkable about the dreams of cult members is their relative absence. Many ex-members report that although they had usually remembered their dreams before joining the cult, they either did not dream or did not remember their dreams during the time they were in the cult. While it is possible that abridged sleep time affects sleep and dream patterns, it is more likely that the need to repress unconscious material felt to be dangerous to life in the cult is responsible for the perceived absence of dreaming. Cult members who do remember their dreams report having nightmares in which they are chased simultaneously by cult members and by their families.

Nightmares are very common among ex-members. One young man told me that he had no recollection of dreams during the entire time he had been in the Unification Church, although he had previously been aware of dreaming and usually remembered his dreams. The very night he left the church—a night he spent with his father in a motel—he had a nightmare in which cult members were pursuing him.

Another ex-member told me of a series of nightmares she experienced that concerned her own struggle to free herself from the group. She would dream that she had left, and then suddenly, to her panic, she'd find herself back in.

Psychiatrist and cult watcher Dr. John Clark reports that ex-members have more than the normal number of nightmares, many of which are about their past in the cult. He also thinks that cult members frequently experience what has been called "black sleep," sleep without dreams or without the usual form of dreams. Experiencing black sleep is like falling into utter blackness, into a pit, and coming out of it with a start, without any consciousness of even having been asleep.[3]

It would be interesting to know if and how the dreams of Germans changed in the latter years of the Reich. From what little we do know about the dreams of people in extreme situations, it seems probable that dreaming is a survival mechanism. The content of dreams and the ability to remember dreams, or to dream at all, are profoundly influenced by anxiety, and the expression of conflict in dreams occurs only when the dreamer feels relatively safe.

In this context the dreams of concentration camp prisoners are most revealing.[4] Unlike free Germans, or cult members for that matter, prisoners dreamed of happy times in the past and of escape. Because they had nothing more to protect, nothing more to lose, the self-censoring mechanism in the dream process had relaxed, and they were freed to dream without constraint. Perhaps, too, their dreams gave them some small measure of hope and strength, enhancing their chances for survival.

The experience of members of the more ruthless cults can also be compared with that of people imprisoned in concentration camps. For life in the camps constituted the systematic attempt to break the individual, to destroy his former identity, and to create in him childlike reactions and dependencies.

Breaking the individual began on the ride to the camps. It was a voyage from the world of position, status, shared beliefs and behavior into an abyss. As though to impress upon them that the old world was gone and irretrievable, the guards exercised a mindless tyranny over their prisoners, beating and torturing them indiscriminately.

The stripping away of identity continued in the camps: prisoners were addressed in the familiar "du" form, which in ordinary life is used only among intimates and to small children. All titles (so important in German society), all vestiges of position, occupation, and status were thus eliminated at one stroke. Prisoners were reduced to a common humanity, which, under camp conditions, was often humanity at a very low level.

Prisoners were humiliated in many ways. Especially effective was the camp authorities' subversion of the codes of behavior regulating basic biological functions, in particular, eating and defecating, which was performed publicly. The breakdown of highly socialized patterns of behavior undermined the morale of prisoners and symbolized their degradation.

Humiliation performs a similar function in many of the current cults. Begging, lying ("heavenly deception," as the Moonies call it), the betrayal of loyalties and confidences, and sexual prostitution (dubbed "flirty fishing" by the Children of God) are required "tests" of moral worthiness. In reality, they serve to further alienate members from their pasts and to bind them even more closely to the group. Many of these moral tests are downright sadistic. In Lifespring, a group that sells self-help training, clients are pressured to reveal their innermost fears and fantasies and then forced to live them. "If you say you feel like shit, they'll bury you in shit. If you say you feel like people walk all over you, the group will literally walk on you. If you say you're afraid of being locked up, they'll put you in a cage." [5]

What happens in these cults also occurred in the concentration camps. It became harder for prisoners even to imagine returning to the old life and not uncommon for them to identify with their captors. Some of the veteran prisoners would painstakingly obtain old pieces of SS uniforms to sew onto their tattered clothing. Long-term prisoners prided themselves on being as tough as the SS and imitated the Kapos' game of seeing who among them could stand to be beaten the longest without complaining. Others indulged in the fantasy that some of the SS were truly kind and caring, only hiding their sensitivity behind harsh exteriors.[6] This response corresponds roughly to a phenomenon in childhood development in which the young child (the exact age when this occurs is disputed) suddenly identifies with the parent he has hitherto perceived as a large, powerful creature capable of doing terrible things to him. Identifying or "incorporating the aggressor" is one way the small, dependent child copes with overwhelming and possibly destructive power. A parallel phenomenon seems to occur when adults feel similarly threatened and are similarly dependent.

Identification with the SS was the result of both the prisoners' utter dependence on them and the need to impose order on their experience. Punishments, for example, that fell within an "ordinary" frame of reference—a guard's slaps or kicks, which were not unlike the normal abuses of childhood—evoked a far more violent reaction from the prisoners than did severe punishments. That is, they were able to respond to behavior that was familiar. Under camp conditions, however, this response was inappropriate: it was near suicidal. Even though other prisoners scolded their fellows for reacting in a way that might provoke fatal consequences for all of them, the vehement responses persisted nonetheless. Apparently the need to fit experience into meaningful patterns and to be able to respond to it "normally" outweighed all other emotional and rational considerations.

Meaning is crucial to survival. According to some scholars of the concentration camp experience, prisoners who were able to find meaning in the experience were better able to survive it; physically weaker prisoners were often able to endure what sturdier specimens could not. Dissociation was another aid to surviving. One man who as a small boy had been in the camps spoke of having experienced it all as though he had been watching a grotesque movie. He was convinced that his attitude of being a curious spectator had enabled him to survive.

Bruno Bettelheim, himself a survivor of a concentration camp, has remarked on the parallels of behavior between schizophrenic children and the inmates of concentration camps. Both, he explains, felt similarly about their lives, "deprived of hope, and totally at the mercy of destructive irrational forces bent on using [them] for their goals." [7] The symptomatic reactions to life in the camps bore a striking resemblance to clinical schizophrenia and included suicidal tendencies; catatonia, or responding to any demand of the SS with no will of one's own; melancholic depression; infantile behavior; delusions; projections; general loss of memory; shallow, inappropriate emotions; and inability to correctly assess reality.[8] These symptoms are also found among the victims of brainwashing. The common feature among schizophrenic children, concentration camp victims, and people subjected to brainwashing is the feeling of being totally overwhelmed.

One of the conditions that produce schizophrenia is a pattern of behavioral interaction called the double bind. The double bind is also common to many brainwashing situations, and it may account in part for the schizophreniclike reactions in people so subjected.

The anthropologist Gregory Bateson has hypothesized that part of the symptomatology of schizophrenia is a confusion in communication. He maintains that the schizophrenic lacks the ability to properly discriminate "message identifying signals" that are the basic components of all communication. This inability results from having been subjected to a double-bind pattern of communication in a primary relationship during early childhood.

The classic double bind occurs in the family when a mother, for whatever reasons, feels threatened by her child's desire for intimacy with her and reacts to it by withdrawing. At the same time, she cannot face *not* being a "loving mother," and so to shield herself from having to acknowledge it she feigns the role. Yet when her child responds warmly to the pretense, the mother once again withdraws. The bind is created because the mother is compelled both to withdraw and to deny that she is withdrawing.

In consequence, the child is given conflicting messages to which he cannot satisfactorily respond. If he withdraws in reaction to his mother's initial hostility, he is blamed for not loving her and not confirming her need to feel like a loving parent. If he tries to draw closer to her, he is rejected, as well as criticized, for the mother rationalizes her own withdrawal by asserting that the child is not being sincere. There is no way for the child to win. And worse, the burden of an impossible situation is thrown onto the person least able to handle it.

The bind become increasingly convoluted. As Bateson describes it, "the mother uses the child's responses to affirm that her behavior is loving, and since the loving behavior is simulated, the child is placed in the position where he must not accurately interpret her communication if he is to maintain a relationship with her." [9] But this he must do. Because the small child is dependent on his mother, maintaining the relationship is paramount

The price, however, is dear. The child is punished for accurately perceiving what his mother is expressing, and he is also punished for perceiving inaccurately. The child's "solution" is to distort his own perceptions so as to make his reading correspond to his mother's demands. "He must deceive himself about his own internal state to support Mother in her deception. To survive with her, he must falsely discriminate his own internal messages as well as falsely discriminate the messages of others." [10] The solution is to confound the whole process of communication.

The reaction of adults subjected to the double bind is not unlike that of schizophrenic children. After a while, they begin to distort their own responses to information and to confuse different types of information. Because they feel threatened, they lose, for example, the ability to distinguish between humor and seriousness, and, in consequence, many of their responses are inappropriate. Literal messages are confused with metaphorical messages. What occurs is a breakdown in communication, or, as Bateson says, in the "metacommunicative system"—the communication about communication. Unable to determine what sort of message a message is, the person subjected to the double bind retreats into metaphor and denial.

Many of the contemporary cults use the double bind to inculcate dependence and submission. A simple form of it exists in the requirement that members deny certain human impulses within themselves. Calling these desires Satanic is a way of alienating people from themselves. They do not want to be identified with what has been defined as an evil force, nor can they rid themselves totally of basic human reactions. The only real solution for them would be to refute the initial definition, but this solution would provoke a dangerous confrontation with the leaders. It is the classic no-win situation. Cult members, like most Germans under the Third Reich, are intimidated into repressing their own feelings and instincts.

A form of the double bind frequently exists in the relationship cult members have with their leader. Robert Perez, for example, in discussing a typical experience in his cult, unwittingly described the classic double bind. Patterson Brown, the leader of Christ Brotherhood, had mowed the lawn one day. He had been unable, however, to cut a narrow strip of grass that sloped precipitously and was riddled with pot holes. To help out, Robert took a scythe and cut down the tall grass. At that point the Guru became furious, screaming, "You know you should leave it alone! You know that if I didn't cut that, I didn't cut that for a reason. If you only knew what it was like to be a child, you'd know that it's fun to play in the weeds." Needless to say, Robert was taken aback. Criticized for helping, he knew that he would also have been criticized for not helping. "It was the kind of thing that in another frame of mind with him, a week down the line, he'd say, 'How come nobody's done that? Do I have to do everything around here?' "

Christ Brotherhood members never knew what to expect. Each morning they half anticipated to be told to get out and never come back. The unpredictability of their leader, as Robert expressed it, "made you completely paranoid about what you were doing and what you weren't doing. You'd do one thing and then he'd just flip-flop the other way. You never knew if he was going to turn around and yell at you or praise you." Unfortunately, the erratic nature of Christ Brotherhood's leader could not be easily dismissed by his followers because they depended upon him and his opinions to validate their own lives. "What Patterson said was how you felt about yourself. If he said you were a good person, that what you had just done was good, that you were growing and progressing in the discipleship, then you felt good about yourself. If he said you were a creep and a shmuck, you felt like you were a creep and a shmuck."

Like children subjected to the double bind, members of this group distorted their instinctive reactions. Having abdicated autonomy, they also abdicated any independent perception of reality. Once, for example, after a particularly venomous tirade berating cult members for living "like pigs in a fucking dive," their leader sat down with a cigarette and let the ashes drop all over the floor. His followers saw no hypocrisy: "Yes," they told themselves, "we've got to keep this place clean, but Patterson knows that when he points these things out to people, it unleashes very intense energy in the direction of cleanliness and he doesn't want people to be uptight and paranoid about it. That's why he flicks his ashes on the floor."

After he had left the cult, Robert remarked that he could "really identify with those people in the People's Temple who would stand up and say they were homosexuals—that they couldn't have a satisfactory experience with a woman—who were lying about themselves, who were ready to take on an identity that wasn't true. That's what Patterson did to you, too."

Jim Jones was another cult leader whose relationship with followers was characterized by the double bind. Jones's mercurial personality alternated between violent vituperation and paternal affection, keeping his followers on permanent tenterhooks. One of his standard tactics was to cajole a person into publicly revealing a weakness and then, in the middle of the confession, to become contemptuous or bored. Often Jones would abruptly interrupt someone's painful revelation with a demand for food. The person confessing could hardly fault Jones, who had remained ostensibly loving. The implicit message of the interaction, however, was rejection: the personal testimonies of his followers were apparently of less importance to Jones than the banana he craved at that moment. As in all double-bind situations, the burden of the contradiction rested with the person being rejected, and intense dependency prevented that person from questioning the other's behavior.

A deep sense of guilt accompanies the double bind. The child, in the classic example, feels guilty about any internal reservations he harbors about his mother. Similarly, messiahs like Patterson Brown or Jim Jones inculcate guilt among their followers. In Jones's tapes of all the Jonestown happenings, he repeatedly complains that he "gets no joy anymore" because he "worries so much about all of you." He is "willing to die for you," and he wishes he still had the strength to "hold all of you so you never have any more pain." The burden of all this love lay heavily on his followers, who dared not question any demand that Jones might make of them.

One taped interaction at Jonestown recalls a dream that was told to Charlotte Beradt by the owner of a small factory in Germany. The factory owner, in reality a generous employer and proud anti-Fascist, is visited in the dream by Goebbels, who demands that he be saluted Fascist-style. The factory owner wants to refuse, but doesn't dare. The act of raising his arm in front of all his employees, who are aware of his political convictions, is a prolonged, torturous humiliation. Sweat pours down his face and blood streams down the intransigent arm. When he finally manages to salute, Goebbels angrily stomps out.

In the Jonestown sequence, Jones has asked his followers if they are ready to die for him. A soft-spoken man replies, "I'm prepared to die after forty-four years of not being able to contribute anything to this life or find any reason for it at all." As if that is not enough, he is then asked whether he is prepared to take his daughter's life. At that point he resists, answering that he'd happily give his own in place of hers. This resistance angers the others, and the man is berated until he acquiesces that "if the Fascists were coming up the road, I would take her life." At that point, Jones suddenly interjects, announcing in a comforting voice, "Now, people who are really loving and a Father who is genuinely compassionate is prepared for all such emergencies, and the children will be spared." Jones has forced a father to agree to murder his child (in the child's presence, by the way) and then has done an abrupt about-face, declaring that it won't be necessary. Like Goebbels in the factory owner's dream, Jones has demanded and received the ultimate sacrifice, and then tossed it aside like a rag.

Many of the other techniques used by cults have their parallels with the methods employed by the Third Reich. Just as the German SS deliberately separated family members as a way of undermining prisoners, messianic cults try to sever members' contact with their families. Families pose a threat to the messiahs because they represent attachments and loyalties that challenge the leaders' supremacy. And it is no coincidence that cults present themselves as families: the attempt to replace the biological family is an effort to eliminate the competition.

From the moment of entry into a cult, the novice's communication with his or her family is supervised: phone calls are tapped, letters censored, and visits eliminated or chaperoned. Moreover, those who try to maintain close family relations are subjected to pressure and criticism. Rejecting one's family is justified in a number of ways. According to the Unification Church, for instance, everyone outside the church is part of "Satan's world" and thus by implication, Satan's instrument. Other cults justify hating one's parents by distorted reference to the Bible—the only true father is the Holy Father, and the only real parents are spiritual parents. Another way of alienating members from their families is by pressuring novices to obtain contributions from their parents. This tactic frequently antagonizes already estranged relationships. It is a subtle way of subverting loyalties, encouraging cult members to regard their parents as "prey." Most parents of children in cults find they cannot maintain "normal" contact with them. Parental desperation is then used as a means to weaken family ties: told hair-raising stories about abductions and deprogrammings, converts become terrified of any contact with their parents.

Marriages and children also come under fire in the cults. The issue of children is an especially sensitive one, for their very presence contradicts one of the basic premises of cult life: In Heaven there is one Father, one Perfect Parent; all others are his children. It is terribly difficult to behave as responsible parents while actively abdicating adulthood, and children have borne the brunt of this conflict.

Child abuse has been an endemic feature of cults. In the 1930s, public outcry forced Father Divine to issue new directives to his followers—*not* to abandon their children under sixteen years of age. But even then his reversal was qualified. Although forced to order that children be fed, clothed, and given shelter, he continued to maintain that children neither had to be nor indeed should be loved.

Child abuse was a pervasive element in Jonestown. Jim Jones ruthlessly exploited the fears of children in the effort to break their spirit. Fear of the dark, of strange animals, of one's own body, of exposure and sexuality, were used to destroy a child's security, particularly his relationship with his parents. "Bad" children were tied up and left overnight in the jungle; they were dropped into a well where "Big Foot" (followers hidden there) would drag them down into the water. Teenagers were given public beatings: one father tells of watching his daughter's "butt beaten until it looked like hamburger." Others were put into the "extended care unit," where they were drugged and electrically shocked.

The violation of children was especially deadly to their parents. The act of forcing parents to acquiesce to the brutalization of their young was a key means for breaking their integrity and was as well an indication of the disintegration that had already taken place. The routine of asking parents if they were willing to kill their children, presumably a matter of loyalty, in reality symbolized a terrible breakdown of human values.

As a way of handling the conflicts created by the presence of children, some cults maintained that children are communal property. Robert Perez, for example, was required to renounce his son, for Christ Brotherhood does not acknowledge parenthood. "He wasn't my son," Robert said simply, "he was God's son." It was standard policy in Jonestown for parents to sign over legal custody of their children to Jim Jones. This policy served not only as an undermining of family ties, but also as a source of potential blackmail.

Another common practice among cults is to break up the marriages of members. This approach is a double whammy: it attacks a relationship that represents an adult commitment independent of the cult, and it effectively eliminates the problem of children. Robert and Jane Kaufman struggled to maintain their relationship in the face of concerted opposition. "We were trying to stay together," Jane told me, "and then, right before I had the baby, they broke Robert. They just fed him so many lies about me that he decided he wanted to spend some time away from me."

Robert: "They got me to feel that she was the source of all my unhappiness. And I was unhappy at times. I mean I was feeling a high level of tension and frustration that transferred onto her. They'd sit me down and talk to me about her, feeding my fantasy that I already had about myself, about serving the poor, and that the worst thing for me, in terms of a companion, was someone who was self-indulgent and thought only of herself. They kept telling me that I was this sterling character and she was just a selfish shmuck who took advantage of me."

Finally, his loyalties torn, Robert went to Patterson for resolution. The upshot was that Jane was sent away in her eighth month of pregnancy. Holed up in a Christ Brotherhood house in Colorado, and virtually alone, she gave birth to her son. "The period after I had the baby, when I was separated from Robert, was an awful time. It was horrible. I really convinced myself that I was okay on one level, but it was really horrible. I don't remember having any dreams during that period."

One of the chief ways of weakening the marriage bond is by subverting sexuality. In many cults, sex is simply repressed. Messiahs decree sex to be sinful, and marriage partners feel full of conflicts about their desires. Often the shameful option is removed entirely, and spouses are physically separated, sleeping respectively in men's and women's quarters. To discourage sexual urges, cults like Hare Krishna insist that genitalia be tightly bound, while Reverend Moon has his own solution for marriage and sex: his church is famous for mass marriages in which hundreds or thousands of members are simultaneously wedded, often to people they have never met. These marriages are not intended to be flesh and blood relationships; usually they are never consummated. It is commonplace for spouses to live in separate communes. Such marriages are mere symbols, yet they serve important functions: they suit many young Moonies who are unsure of their sexuality and are relieved by these nonsexual marriages, and they allow the church to maintain control over the personal lives of members. As many of these marriages are between Koreans and Americans they allow Moon to bring more Korean Moonies into the United States.

In other cults, sex is perverted. Because marriages are potential threats to a messiah's domination over followers, messiahs frequently encourage sexual philandering within the flock. Some have even required members to play sexual musical chairs. Others use sexual orgies to break down inhibitions. One woman said her cult leader maintained that "if a person didn't feel comfortable in group sex, it indicated a psychological hang-up that had to be stripped away because it prevented us all from melding and unifying."

Some messiahs approach the issue of sexuality in a different manner: they try to corner the market personally. They do not necessarily enter into sexual relationships with members; often they simply encourage sexual feelings from their followers. Many of the rituals in cults, the "testimonies of faith," serve as sexual catharses. The wild buildup of emotion and movement, the sudden release and collapse, mimic sexual orgasm. Usually these displays are directed toward the messiah, who is seen, as Father Divine put it, as "father, husband, and lover rolled into one." I have been told that women have a harder time leaving cults run by male messiahs. Some have reported that even after leaving, they would fantasize about the messiah while engaged in sexual intercourse.

The subversion of sexuality is used to break up marriages, but it is far more potent a weapon. So much of our adult persona is tied up with our sexuality. To tamper with it is to tamper with our deep and hidden selves. It is no wonder then that virtually all of the current cults seek to harness that power.

Jim Jones, for example, deliberately sabotaged the sexual identity of his followers: husbands were obliged to declare themselves homosexuals; wives publicly announced that their husbands physically disgusted them; and parents confessed to sexually violating their children. Jones also tried to establish a sexual monopoly in his commune, servicing his "children," willing or unwilling. Sex was power, as far as he was concerned. He used it to break down his followers, to destroy marriages, and to force men and women to submit to his will.

Double binding, the weakening of family relationships, and the subversion of sexuality are all ways of undermining integrity and autonomy. They weaken resistance to outside influences, creating in the individual the state of dependency necessary for maintaining indoctrination. The indoctrination practices of the Unification Church or the People's Temple, for example, are simply variations on a very old theme. Though differing in detail and in intensity, their result is to create an environment in which self-expression and dissent are impossible, if not dangerous. In these cults, as in the Third Reich, safety rests in utter conformity—in self-abnegation. The fate of individuals subjected to this environment is expressed simply in the following dream of a German woman in 1933: "In place of the street signs which had been abolished, posters had been set up on every corner, proclaiming in white letters on a black background the twenty words people were not allowed to say. The first was *Lord*—to be on the safe side I must have dreamt it in English. I don't recall the following words and possibly didn't even dream them, but the last one was *I*."

7 ≡

THE PHYSIOLOGY
OF BRAINWASHING

What are the physical effects of brainwashing? Some of the side effects that cult membership commonly produces—disturbances in perception, memory, and other information processes; the cessation of menstruation in women and the absence of facial hair growth among men—indicate that brainwashing or coercive indoctrination is not just a matter of psychological manipulation, but affects the central nervous system as well.

It is hard to substantiate any specific impairment of brain function, for very little is known about the complex processes of cognition and higher mental functioning that are particularly vulnerable to brainwashing. The brain is, in fact, the scientific new world, still largely unexplored and uncharted. What is known about brain development and function, however, suggests some speculative approaches to understanding the physiological component of brainwashing.

Above all, brainwashing affects one's identity. And one's identity is inextricably bound to the way one's brain evolves and operates. Who we are is a reflection of the interplay between our brains and the outside world. It is an ongoing relationship, beginning during gestation and continuing throughout our lives.

Human beings are not born completely formed. The essential element that distinguishes humans from the lower animals is the neocortex, the area of the brain responsible for coordination and higher mental abilities. At birth, the neocortex is barely developed; in fact, 85 percent of brain growth occurs after birth.

The neocortex develops gradually, in response to its environment. Its growth depends on stimulation from outside; it develops in reaction to information bombarding the infant. In response to this information, the anatomical structure and the biochemistry of the neocortex are formed: the connections between nerve cells (neurons) and the synapses (the points of communication between neurons) become established. The growth of human intellectual capacity corresponds to the physical development of the brain, which in turn depends upon contact with the outside environment.

The infant's dependency on its environment makes it vulnerable. Certain periods are especially critical to brain development. During the first eighteen months of life, for example, if the child is deprived of protein or information—the essential nutrients for brain growth—its brain can be permanently impaired. Kwashiorkor, a disease caused by chronic protein deficiency, is extremely common, reducing the learning potential of seven out of ten children under age six throughout the world.

The absence or paucity of sensory information also impairs brain growth. Experiments performed on young rats reared in conditions akin to solitary confinement damaged their brain structure and size. Control rats, raised in an "enriched" environment (they lived in groups, were given plenty of toys, and were frequently handled) developed thicker cerebral cortexes than their deprived fellows. As little as an hour a day of "enriched" experience caused measurable differences in their brains.[1] *

Even after the brain reaches its full growth (between ages eleven and fourteen) the environment continues to play a pivotal role. According to neurophysiologist Steven Rose, "The extent to which brain structure and biochemistry is state-dependent, being continually modified in response to changed environmental circumstances, is only now becoming apparent. Clearly it is always necessary to consider the brain as part of a system which includes all aspects of the environment of that brain."

The extreme interdependence of the brain and its environment means that a radical change in the environment will affect the workings of the brain. This has important implications for the study of brainwashing. The process becomes, if not totally understood, at least theoretically implied. Any discussion of brainwashing, then, must take into consideration the way the brain processes information.

The brain is a complex communication system. It receives, processes, and emits information. The primary "tools" used to perform this task are the neurons. There are some hundred billion neurons in the human brain and between ten thousand million and one hundred thousand million neurons in the cere-

---

* Another experiment, of dubious authenticity, performed in the thirteenth century, yielded more startling results. Conducted by Frederick II, King of Sicily and Emperor of the Holy Roman Empire, its purpose was to discover which language infants would speak spontaneously if raised in a verbal vacuum. Would they speak Hebrew, the oldest known language, or Greek or Arabic or perhaps the language of their natural parents? He gathered a random sample of infants, instructing foster mothers to feed and bathe them, but not to talk to them. Unfortunately, Frederick never discovered what the "natural" human language was, for all his subjects died before uttering a word.

bral cortex alone. In each square millimeter of cortical surface are one hundred thousand neurons.[2]

Each neuron is composed of a cell body, a major fiber called the axon, and a number of branches called the dendrites. Neurons communicate with each other via the synapse, the tiny gap at the end of the axon. The synapse transmits signals, which are received by the dendrites and the cell body. The cell body combines and integrates these signals and then emits outgoing signals. The axon transports the outgoing signal to the axon terminal, which passes the information across the synapse, where it is received by the dendrites of the next neuron.

The means of this communication is both electrical and chemical. The signal generated by a neuron and carried along its axon is electrical. At the synapse, the electrical signal is transformed into a chemical transmitter substance, which bridges the synaptic gap between neurons. It flows across the synapse, where it is received by a dendrite.* The message then travels, once again in the form of an electrical signal, down the dendrite into the cell body of the second neuron.

Synapses do not just automatically transmit signals. Rather they are points of determination that can inhibit as well as excite the neuron next in line, thus influencing how that neuron responds. What happens to a signal or piece of information is determined largely by the relationship between the chemical transmitter substance produced by the first neuron, at the synapse, and the chemical nature of the receiving neuron's membrane at the other side of the synapse. The fate of the signal also depends upon the sum total of all the other signals the second neuron is receiving at the same time. For each neuron is fed by hundreds or thousands of other neurons, and its response to any

---

* It can also be received by a cell body, or occasionally an axon terminal.[3]

given signal reflects that entire input. Each neuron evaluates all the signals reaching it from other neurons and expresses the result through its own rate of electrical firing or signaling.

This description is oversimplified. The transactions made at the synapses are enormously complex. Just how complex is indicated by the estimate that in a single human cortex there are 10^{14} synaptic contacts, or thirty thousand times as many synapses as there are people in the world.

Scientists believe the synapses are the tools for processing information, providing the brain with the possibility of coding, classifying, and operating on information arriving at it from the outside. Steven Rose, among other neurophysiologists, maintains that it is the synapse that accounts for the qualities that make us human. "At the synapse between cells lies the choice point which converts the nervous system from a certain, predictable and dull one into an uncertain, probabilistic and hence interesting system. Consciousness, learning and intelligence are all synapse-dependent. It is not too strong to say that the evolution of humanity followed the evolution of the synapse."

The very plasticity of the operations of the synapse has implications for brainwashing. Synaptic patterns develop in response to a relatively consistent set of information derived from an individual's life experiences and environment. Radical changes in that information base upset established synaptic patterns and result in changed behavior. The techniques of brainwashing take advantage of this highly adaptable system. In fact, brainwashing represents a repatterning of synaptic operations, affecting the way the brain processes information. Brainwashing techniques specifically focus on the memory functions, requiring individuals to commit to memory large amounts of new information and to reprocess old information. Memory, more than anything else, is the essence of personal identity; it shapes the individual. The vulnerability of the individual's memory to manipulation is one of the brainwasher's most potent tools. An understanding of the physiological processes involved in learning should indicate how these processes can be affected by brainwashing.

Such understanding is not easy to come by, for memory is the subject of much scientific controversy. No one is entirely sure what memory is, whether it is electrical or biochemical in nature, and where in the brain it is located and stored. Much, however, is known. Memory involves three processes: learning, remembering, and forgetting. Obviously, something must first be learned before it becomes a memory. The process of transforming newly learned information into a memory, which can later be recalled, takes time. Pavlov, in his famous experiments, taught dogs to associate the sound of a bell with food. The effectiveness of the lesson was measured by the amount of salivation (the involuntary response to food) produced by the sound of the bell. Shortly after he had conditioned a group of dogs, Leningrad was flooded. The dogs were rescued at the last minute, for water had nearly filled their cages. Retesting the dogs shortly after their rescue revealed that they had forgotten the conditioned response to the bell. The phenomenon of forgetting newly learned information after sudden shock has been replicated in scientifically controlled experiments. War shock, too, yields the same result. Memories of events immediately preceding a bombing are often irretrievably lost. What these accidents and experiments have proven is that it takes time to commit learning to the permanent memory store—in fact, between thirty minutes and three hours. If this process is interrupted by a traumatic event, it is quite likely that the learned information will not become a memory.

There are qualitative differences between long-term and

short-term memories. The fixing process occurring with long-term memories seems to involve a biochemical transformation, whereas short-term memories (memories retained for a very short period and then forgotten) constitute a different process and involve different areas of the brain. It appears, then, that learning is a flexible, open-ended series of actions and reactions over time. Decisions must be made whether to commit new information to long-term or short-term storage. Furthermore, the process of fixing memories is vulnerable to external influence.

Researchers have assumed that "learning represents the opening of new functional pathways within the brain." Pavlov's experiments illustrate this. Salivation upon the presentation of food is an involuntary response; it is a wired-in reflex, like the knee jerk. This reflex may involve a simple neuronal pathway. The association learned by repeatedly following the sound of the bell with the presentation of food eventually produces a learned reflex represented by a new pathway that connects bell sound with salivation. It follows that the memory itself is the new pathway formed as a result of the conditioning, and that each memory is "coded for in some way by a unique pathway."

No one knows, however, what physical form memories really take. Some scientists have speculated that the memory pathways take physical shape in the dendrites. The problem with this explanation, even as speculation, is space. If dendrites were physical forms of memory, the brain would become hopelessly clogged with dendritic connections, since learning never stops.

An alternative explanation, one that enjoys a great deal of support, is that learning or memory involves biochemical changes at the synapses. This idea is supported, indirectly, by experiments indicating that the production of protein and RNA (the template on which protein is made in the cell) is increased during learning. That there is an association between learning, synaptic modifications, and protein synthesis is suggested by studies that have found changes in the sizes and numbers of synapses and in the rates of protein synthesis in the same areas of the brain after the introduction of a new external stimulus. For example, electron micrograph studies of rats reared in the dark but exposed to light immediately before being killed have shown changes in the synapses of their visual cortex, lateral geniculate (brain region of the ascending optic pathway), and retinas, as well as changes in protein synthesis of those same areas. In other words, the learning process apparently involves anatomical change and increased protein synthesis.

This association between enhanced protein synthesis and learning has also been suggested in experiments directed to the "imprinting" response in newborn chicks. At the moment of hatching, chicks are genetically programmed to follow any moving object. Within an hour after chicks were exposed to an imprinting stimulus, scientists found increases in the production of RNA. Within two hours, they discovered an increased production of protein.

Other experiments tested this association by injecting animals with drugs that suppress protein synthesis just before or after a learning experience. The injected animals did not remember what they had learned. A control group, injected with a placebo, did. Though not conclusive, these and other experiments reinforce the notion that protein synthesis is crucial to the fixation of information into long-term memory. This would explain why protein deficiencies during the early stages of brain growth in children result in damage to their subsequent learning capacity. It also provides a clue to understanding the deleterious effects of brainwashing on memory. Moreover, there is evidence, to be discussed shortly, that certain types of stress also affect the rate of protein synthesis.

Even if it may be assumed that learning involves synaptic

changes, the question regarding the localization of memory remains. Given the fact that 10^4 neurons die each day, it would appear that memory cannot be located in only one network of synaptic connections. Moreover, experiments designed to discover the location of memory by surgically removing portions of an animal's brain have failed to eliminate memories. Neurologist Karl Lashley performed a series of such experiments on rats after they had learned to navigate a maze. Despite radical surgery and resulting motor impairments, Lashley's subjects managed, somehow, to get through the maze. In another group of experiments whose objective was to locate memory, Canadian neurosurgeon Wilder Penfield used electrical probes on humans suffering from neurological disorders. Contrary to Lashley's findings, Penfield's experiments indicated that specific areas of the brain were associated with specific memories and that the repeated electrical stimulation of a particular area consistently evoked a particular memory.

The seeming discrepancy between these two sets of experiments can be accounted for by another characteristic of the brain: redundancy. There are many duplicate pathways for the transmission of information. Within the brain, there are probably many tens of thousands of cells that perform the same tasks. Thus, although memory is coded in a particular network of synaptic connections, the network itself is most likely duplicated in different parts of the cortex and in both brain hemispheres. Memory, in other words, is simultaneously localized and diffuse.

In speculating on how memory works, neurophysiologist Karl Pribram has compared the mechanism of memory storage to a hologram. Holography is a photographic method that uses laser beams to produce three-dimensional images by splitting the beam in two and recording on a photographic plate the interference patterns formed when the beams converge. One beam is projected directly onto the plate; the other is reflected off the object being photographed. When a third beam of laser light illuminates the developed film, the original three-dimensional image is produced. Moreover, if the developed film is cut into pieces, each fragment, when illuminated, will produce the entire image.

The image of the hologram illustrates the distributed character of memory and, most particularly, the potential of a detail to evoke an entire recollection. There is also another feature of the hologram that bears analogy to the brain: the information recorded in the hologram is projected from the object being photographed as well as onto it—just as the receipt of information by the brain depends upon the interaction between the incoming information and the already existing organizational patterns within the brain.

How memories are recalled poses another set of problems. Some crucial questions in this regard are: Why is it easy to remember the alphabet in the normal order but hard to say it backward? Why is it hard or perhaps impossible to recognize a tune hummed backward? And why, if you stop the flow of a memory in midstream, is it hard to resume or even recollect the flow later on? The physiological character of synaptic firing helps to explain this phenomenon. Memory is sequential, because synapses conduct electrical messages from the neuron in an orderly progression. The firing of an axon, too, is sequential. The axon must fire before a synapse can conduct information to an adjacent neuron, which then fires, activates a response at yet another synapse, and so on. The physical path of information corresponds to the way memories are recalled: one association leads to another. Thus, the decision to remember a particular event is determined by an already existing state of mind. "The act of choosing," to quote Steven Rose, "is itself programmed by the firing of particular cells; a 'prestate' is necessary before the brain state relevant to a particular memory can be achieved."

Forgetting is the third process associated with memory. It is difficult to know just why we forget and whether forgetting represents a temporary or permanent loss of memory. There are several possible causes of forgetting. One is that an old memory becomes overshadowed by new information. The brain's capacity for conscious concentration is very limited, especially in proportion to the amount of continuous information processing and interpretation that occurs without our conscious awareness. Given this economy, it is logical that more immediately relevant information will supersede less useful information.

Another reason we forget is that information is deliberately suppressed. The blocking of information can be described in biological terms as cellular restraints that prevent firing patterns corresponding to specific memories. Some constraints are built into the system, for without any control over the release of memories, meaningful organization of information is not possible.

There are cases, however, of individuals who lacked such constraints. The Russian neurologist A. R. Luria documented the case of S., who was unable to forget anything he had ever experienced. S.'s memory was totally nonselective, a "junk heap of impressions"; he remembered everything, however trivial. The consequence for S. was tragic, for he was unable to function normally, unable to hold even a simple job. Everything he heard or saw set up uncontrollable chains of recollections, and he could not organize information or assign priorities to it.[4]

Apart from the "normal" cellular restraints (which individuals like S. appear to lack), the blocking of information can be induced by other factors, notably stress. Stress prevents certain memories from occurring by producing a biochemical chain reaction that alters ordinary firing patterns.

This blockage, of course, has implications for brainwashing. Tampering with the memory process very likely leads to the alterations in personality observed in people who have been brainwashed.

Stress is the key factor in brainwashing or coercive indoctrination. This was evident after the Korean conflict when relatives of American servicemen who had been prisoners of war found them strange and "different" when they returned home. Parents of cult members have much the same reaction to their estranged daughters and sons. Individuals are placed in an alien environment, where they are presented with large amounts of new information they are expected to assimilate quickly. The sheer volume of information constitutes a stress that very probably disrupts the complex biochemical and electrical circuitry of the memory processes. The consequences of failing to learn all the information, however, represent other kinds of stress—fear and anxiety. At the same time, during indoctrination sleep and nutrition patterns are altered in such a way as to impede further the learning process.

The neurophysiological consequences of brainwashing on the memory processes may be inferred from what is known about stress. Although its precise mechanisms are not known, there is circumstantial evidence that stress affects several related processes: the protein synthesis in the neurons associated with learning; the biochemical transmitters at the synapses, which are responsible for passing or inhibiting the flow of messages; the hormonal levels, which alter the brain's chemistry; and the reticular formation responsible for alertness and the arousal level of the brain. The reticular formation, in particular, appears to be directly involved in the organization and assessment of incoming sensory information. Signals from the reticular formation (located in the brain stem) alert the cortex, at the appropriate times, to pay attention to incoming information, and stress may interfere with the capability of the reticular formation to integrate and evaluate sensory input. Stress, in other words, alters the brain's receptivity to new information, the ability to remember old information, and the capacity to integrate information.

Similar behavioral patterns have been observed in people subjected to a variety of stressful situations. People in sensory restriction experiments, in indoctrination situations, in concentration camps, and under the influence of certain drugs have all manifested a common set of symptoms. Of these four situations, experiments in sensory restriction shed most light on the physiological mechanism of stress, for they are relatively free from the emotionality that characterizes the three others. Sensory restriction experiments are of two types: sensory deprivation, in which an attempt is made to reduce sensory stimulation to the absolute minimum; and perceptual deprivation, in which an attempt is made to reduce the patterning and meaningful organization of sensory input while maintaining a somewhat normal level of input.[5]

A large literature of sensory restriction studies has shown that the limitation of sensory input, whether it involves the total elimination of sensation (sensory isolation) or just the restriction of information, results in impaired cortical functions. The brain is dependent on the outside world for orientation. If one is deprived of this contact, even temporarily, one's behavior rapidly becomes disturbed—so disturbed at times as to resemble psychosis. Dr. Marvin Zuckerman has reported a series of effects typical of the sensory restriction experiments. They include difficulties in directed thinking and concentration; a drifting of thoughts toward fantasies and daydreams; disorientation in time; body illusions and delusions; somatic discomforts—headaches, backaches, pains in the neck and eyes; paranoidlike delusions and hallucinations.

Hallucinations occur frequently in situations in which sensory flow is restricted. Survivors of shipwrecks adrift on the open sea, for example, report that after a period of initial terror, they began to hallucinate. In sensory deprivation experiments reported by Dr. Jay Shurley [6] and others hallucinations occur within a few hours. One of Dr. Shurley's subjects saw "a field of golden toadstools with sunlight brightly reflected from the stem of one." Another "felt that I was stirring with my left leg, and it was a spoon in an iced-tea glass, just going round and round." Donald Hebb, who pioneered some of the early water-tank immersion experiments, observes, "if one is alone long enough, and at levels of physical and human stimulation low enough, the mind turns inward and projects outward its own contents and processes." [7] It is as though the brain were a stomach, which, deprived of food, begins to cannibalize itself.

The lack of incoming sensation apparently affects the reticular formation. The resulting behavioral symptoms point to a breakdown of the intricate control mechanisms that filter and transmit sensory information. The "psychotic" experiences reported indicate the disorientation to which even quite healthy brains succumb under situations of stress.*

Mental disturbances resulting from sensory restriction show up in the electroencephalogram (EEG) frequencies of subjects.

---

* The work of Mendelson and others suggests that some forms of sensory restriction also affect levels of certain biochemical substances, including norepinephrine, one of the transmitter substances of the synapses.[8]

Slow brain waves, like those usually associated with sleep, result from a low arousal level due to the low level of sensory variation. Interestingly, the electrical activity of the brain shows greater disturbance under conditions of perceptual deprivation than from total sensory deprivation, which implies that the critical factor is variety, rather than quantity, of sensory input. Moreover, the slowing down of brain waves and the corresponding behavioral effects persist for some time after the experiment and after the subject has returned to a normal sensory environment.

Hallucinating under experimental conditions has been described as dreaming while awake. Despite the sleeplike rate of EEG tracings, hallucinating subjects report that they are conscious. During sleep, the controls that monitor the triggering of memory sequences are lowered, and perhaps the "random" or relatively undirected firing of these sequences accounts for the phenomenon of dreaming. It may be that in situations of imposed sensory restriction a similar lowering of controls occurs and subjects become consciously aware of mental activity that ordinarily occurs only during sleep. An alternative hypothesis is that the lowering of controls causes subjects to become conscious of mental activity that, in fact, occurs constantly without our being aware of it. Very possibly, then, it is the phenomenon of slow brain waves that underlies not only dreaming but also the experience of mystics, the subjects of sensory restriction experiments, and the users of hallucinogenic substances like LSD.

Some experiments have attempted to measure the effect of sensory restriction on cognitive abilities. Subjects have been given intelligence tests before, during, and after the experiment, with results indicating that sensory restriction impairs complicated intellectual tasks but not necessarily activities that are routine and simple. Perceptual deprivation disrupts cognitive function more radically than total sensory deprivation, which is hardly surprising given that it causes a greater disruption of the brain's electrical activity.[9] As would be expected, too, the impairments suffered increase in proportion to the duration of the experiment.

Tests that examined the cognitive effects of sensory overload showed that while sensory overload had a deteriorating effect on long-term memory, it enhanced short-term learning.[10] Accounts of bombing raids in wartime indirectly reinforce these findings. Survivors often acted idiotically cheerful, as though nothing of consequence had occurred. The term *bomb happy*, according to the British physician William Sargant, who treated innumerable war neuroses during World War II, "perfectly described how a bombing, with its consequent fear reactions, could destroy the power of integrated thinking about the past, present, or future in survivors who caught the full brunt."

Another finding with important bearing on brainwashing demonstrates that both sensory overload and sensory deprivation increase the suggestibility of subjects. Sargant remarks that "brain exhaustion [sensory overload] led them [Londoners] to believe stories about 'Lord Haw-Haw's' [propaganda] broadcasts from Germany which they would have at once rejected as untrue when in a more relaxed and less exhausted state." Controlled tests confirm this. Researcher Peter Suedfeld writes, "The data indicate that this phenomenon [increased suggestibility and persuadability] originates with lack of informational anchors in the sensory deprivation situation; the subject is at loose ends, without guidelines for his behavior, unable to concentrate, and in a state of stimulus and information hunger. . . . *This condition has the effect of maximizing the reward value of whatever information is made available to him.*"[11]

Later experiments showed that the experience of sensory deprivation alone may undermine a person's beliefs, whether or not alternative beliefs are presented to him. The increased suggestibility of deprived subjects, then, is a reflection both of the impaired ability to evaluate complex material and of the stimulus hunger that results in the propensity to accept new material indiscriminately. A rough analogy would be that of a rich man who can eat at any restaurant and order whatever suits his fancy. Each day's choice will involve rather complicated decisions and evaluations: what he ate the night before; the particular specialty of the restaurant; the number of calories he feels like tackling; whether his meal will be followed by entertainment, work, or sleep; whether he wishes to impress his companions with the sophistication of his choice or please the waiter with the expense of it. Starve that man for a few days and suddenly even a habitually despised food may acquire unexpected appeal. In time, if his diet remains restricted, due to financial losses or medical orders, his entire thinking about food—what is seen as desirable or intolerable, his priorities and assessments—will change. In a similar fashion, people in cults, or the subjects of sensory restriction experiments, also experience a mental reorganization.

Survivors of shipwrecks, for example, report that the initial onslaught of terror, hallucinations, paranoia, and suicidal and murderous impulses is followed by a period of relative peace. After a few weeks of exposure, for those who survive it, a new security and a new mental integration occur. Survivors, in other words, come to terms with their situation. In fact, once they are rescued, readjustment to ordinary life is often quite difficult for them. John C. Lilly, writing about the sensory deprivation experiments involving immersion in a water tank, observes that if exposure is prolonged and opportunities for reestablishing contact with external reality are lacking, an internal reorganization ultimately will take place, though "how reversibly and how permanently, we do not yet know." [12] The healthy human brain, as brainwashers learned long ago, is highly adaptable and will reorient itself in relation to its environment.

The inability to concentrate, the difficulty in thought organization, the increased suggestibility and concomitant physical complaints are found not only in controlled scientific experiments but in naturally occurring situations of social isolation, including many far less extreme than shipwrecks. Scientific researchers at Antarctic stations confined together for months in a limited space experienced many of the same symptoms—headaches, insomnia, impaired memory, diminished alertness, and inability to concentrate. These symptoms were the result of the "sameness" of their life. This finding corroborates what we know about the mechanism of brain arousal and function. In what is known as the "habituation response," neurons will temporarily cease to fire in response to a monotonous stimulus. In fact, all three categories of sensory disruption—the absence of sensory input, the bombardment of sensory input, and monotonously repeated sensory input—interfere with the activity of the reticular formation and have similar behavioral consequences.

Drugs constitute another form of stress that results in radically disrupted behavior. Toxic chemicals, including some produced by the brain itself, have been known to cause cerebral disorders whose manifestations include psychotic symptoms. According to recent research, drugs that act on the brain can "alleviate the symptoms of depression, mania, and schizophrenia as well as create them. Such drugs act specifically on synaptic processes." [13] The technique of lowering or raising levels of synaptic transmitters by the use of drugs has substantiated the hypothesis that some forms of mental disturbance are the result of excesses or deficiencies of these transmitters or other transmitters that interact with them. Amphetamine, for example, gives rise to a toxic psychosis that closely resembles schizophrenia. The drug increases the level of the transmitter dopamine at the synapse, and although there is no clear evidence of an excess of dopamine among schizophrenics, drugs that lower the level of the activity of dopamine synapses seem to alleviate schizophrenic symptoms.[14] "Normal" behavior depends upon the maintenance of a delicate chemical balance in the brain. "Perfectly tuned and smoothly functioning synapses are essential to the successful operation of such complex mental processes as perception, cognition, affect and judgment." [15]

The theoretical implications of these discoveries are relevant to the study of brainwashing. Very likely, some forms of stress act as toxins in the brain. There is evidence that stress interferes with protein synthesis and synaptic function, both of which are intimately connected with learning and memory as well as with other forms of behavior. The extreme delicacy of the synaptic processes makes them vulnerable to outside interference.

Sleep is another important factor in maintaining the chemical balance in the brain. Some of the same neurotransmitters affected by drugs are also associated with the biology of sleep and dreaming. In recent years, sleep researchers have discovered that there are two different kinds of sleep normally occurring in alternating cycles throughout the sleep period: REM sleep, the sleep characterized by rapid eye movements and by ordinary dreaming, and non-REM sleep, where, as the name suggests, these activities are absent.

Most adults spent about 25 percent of their total sleep period in REM sleep and 75 percent in non-REM sleep. In infants, however, these proportions are different. The newborn spends at least 50 percent of his total sleep time in REM sleep, and the unborn infant (in utero) an even greater proportion. These and other factors have led to speculation that REM sleep is a form of internal stimulation that provides large quantities of excitement to the higher brain centers and is essential for the growth of the central nervous system.[16]

The hypothesis that REM sleep may be involved in cortical functioning is bolstered by the association of the neurotransmitters norepinephrine and serotonin with the REM and non-REM sleep, respectively. Norepinephrine seems to regulate REM sleep—blocking muscular activity and unblocking fast cortical activity. Serotonin, which triggers non-REM sleep, has the opposite effect.

It has also been found that protein synthesis drops during non-REM sleep and increases during REM sleep. These findings have stimulated experiments testing the relationship between REM sleep and the memory processes. A number of researchers appear to have demonstrated a consistent relationship between REM-sleep amounts and the ability to learn and retain new and difficult tasks. It has been shown, for example, that aphasic patients (who have lost their speech abilities due to strokes, etc.), who are relearning to talk, spend a higher proportion of their total sleep time in REM sleep than patients who are not recovering their speech functions.

Other studies have demonstrated that the proportion of REM sleep increases when a subject is confronted with complex, novel, or stressful input. Subjects learning to wear prismatic glasses that reversed the visual field, for example, spent a greater amount of time in REM sleep during the initial period of adjustment. After they became used to the glasses and things started to look normal again, the amount of time they spent in REM sleep dropped back to normal. REM sleep seems to play an especially important role in coping with stress. A number of experimenters have reported a significant relationship between traumatic experiences and an increased proportion of time in REM sleep. It has been speculated that REM sleep helps subjects face up to and adapt to reality.

However conjectural, these findings do reinforce the correlations between the memory processes, protein synthesis, and neurotransmitter substances, pinpointing the role of stress in this complex system. The most ambitious attempt to link together the findings of sleep research is the theory of E. Hartmann. Hartmann's theory maintains that REM sleep restores our mental functioning after a day's work; it helps to consolidate memory and other cognitive abilities and it elevates mood, thus facilitating an emotional and intellectual adaptation to the outside world. It accomplishes this by permitting replenishment of norepinephrine and dopamine, which have become depleted in the course of daytime activities. These substances are presumed to play a critical role in adaptive functioning—in learning, memory, vigilance, and attention. Hartmann further postulates that the levels of dopamine and norepinephrine vary inversely with the need for REM—or what he calls "REM pressure." Thus, drugs that raise the level of these substances lower the need for REM sleep, and vice versa.

These correlations point to another physiological aspect of brainwashing: the disruption of sleep patterns. A combination of stress (which theoretically increases the need for REM sleep) and sleep disruption (especially if it results in REM-sleep deprivation) would appear to be a potent physiological weapon. The changed behavior of brainwashed subjects, and in particular, their inability to concentrate and remember, may thus in part perhaps be attributed to biochemical changes resulting from the manipulation of sleep.

In cults, complex thought processes come under fire. In addition to experiencing the physiological consequences of stress, members are subjected to conditioning techniques that interfere with cognitive functioning. Unlike a traditional rite of passage, for example, which utilizes similar techniques to suspend temporarily ordinary thought processes, many of the current cults not only prolong the stress, which interferes with cognitive capabilities, but teach their subjects methods that stop thinking. The technique of repetitive chanting is a conditioning device that alters neocortical functioning. Used as a means to banish doubts (or, as the cults would have it, to banish Satan), it is very likely a biofeedback technique that alters the electrical activity of the brain, producing a "hypnagogic," or trance, state. This state is defined by the slow brain waves (like those usually associated with sleep) that are the consequences of the low arousal level of the brain resulting from the low level of incoming sensory variation. The trance state reflects a disturbance in the reticular formation and accounts for the difficulty in evaluating information. Trance can become a conditioned pattern of brain activity and may occur even in the absence of the stress that originally provoked it. Rhythmic stimulation—dancing, singing, chanting—can induce it. Among cult members, self-induced trance is a way of calming disturbing thoughts and of censoring the mind when it begins to behave normally. Trance cuts off the input of sensory information, which the normal brain requires for proper functioning. It may be, too, that the prolongation of the trance state ultimately results in basic physiological and personality changes.

Without doubt, brainwashing impairs neocortical functioning. If the self is the sum total of all brain activity—the highly complex interplay between the individual and his environment—a radical disruption of that environment will disrupt the entire system. The litany of symptoms resulting from various situations of stress—the inability to remember, to concentrate, to evaluate information, and the concomitant personality changes—are pathological evidence of this reality.

Psychiatrist John Clark, who has treated many cult members, has theorized about what happens to the mind of the "convert" to produce radical alterations in personality. His theory, though not strictly scientific, is compelling, and it provides another perspective to understanding the physiological effects of brainwashing.

> In cults, people are presented with stressful circumstances, especially huge loads of new information at times in their lives when they are vulnerable, and they dissociate. What the Moonies and the Krishnas and the Scientologists and all the other dangerous cults do is to maintain the dissociation. They keep the parts of the mind—the connections inside the central nervous system—divided in function, in action, and in their connection with the outer world. It's a way of controlling them, and the longer it goes on, the further apart all of this gets to be—like the chronic schizophrenic.[17]

Clark believes it is a "heroic feat of the brain—of the central nervous system" to maintain a single personality. "By the time we grow up, there are so many memory systems within us, that it is a miracle that we maintain a consistently identifiable personality." The advantages of a single personality are obvious. Social animals must be identifiable to other members of the group, and they've got to be reliable. The pressure to be identifiable can be explained as an evolutionary development in social animals: "If at first you're one personality and then another, you're bizarre, nobody can deal with you, and you can't be trusted. You've got to be almost stupidly single to be part of the group, and that's survival."

Clark postulates that in the brain there is a specific mechanism whose function is to maintain a single, clearly identifiable personality. Part of the job of this mechanism is to screen out information that would interfere with keeping the personality so "stupidly single." This mechanism is related to what we call "consciousness" or the "mind." Dr. Clark has likened consciousness to the timer mechanism of any complex computer—the regulator that times and modulates what goes on inside the machine so that it will not be chaotic. He suggests that the flow of information in the brain resembles the competition for attention that occurs in a classroom when many students raise their hands at once:

> Information is embedded in all parts of the brain, and it is reaching for recognition all the time. But there is a counter-searching, a put-your-hands-down, that occurs simultaneously. Most of what comes into our perceptual organs, most of the hands-up pieces of information, is kept out of sight. The regulatory mechanism, the "black box" or consciousness, is responsible for sustaining a normal level of awareness, of interconnectedness in all the parts of the brain. But this mechanism, to continue the computer analogy, is really software. It can be tampered with.

What happens during indoctrination is that the mechanism described by Clark is upset. The onslaught of new information in a situation where old information is absent or repudiated produces problems in identity. If there is no letup from this stress, ultimately the brain adapts to its new environment. This results in an often dramatic change of personality. This problem has often been observed in military personnel and journalists assigned overseas for long periods of time. When they try to retain too much information in the forefront of their minds over too long a period and in foreign circumstances, many of them develop very serious nervous symptoms, including massive breakdown.

The natural ability of the human organism to achieve radical change in a very short period of time leaves it vulnerable to manipulation. Cults exploit this vulnerability, placing potential converts in situations of tremendous stress. The converts are bombarded with unfamiliar kinds and amounts of information, cut off from their own world, and deprived of adequate protein, sleep, and dream time. In consequence, they crack, or dissociate, and the brain's ability to regulate and interpret information becomes severely disrupted. Like the subjects of sensory restriction experiments, potential converts are very suggestible at this point. The moment the Chinese have dubbed "tail cutting" has arrived.

There is an explosive element to the "new" personality. Years ago, psychiatrist Robert Lifton observed in China that people subjected to unrelenting pressure "began to exist on a level that was neither sleep nor wakefulness, but rather an in-between hypnagogic state." In this state, they "were susceptible to destructive and aggressive impulses arising from within themselves." [18] This state is common to cult members as well. A growing number of cult-related suicides and unexplained deaths has been reported. There have been at least five deaths among the Moonies, the most dramatic being the young man who tied himself to the railroad tracks in Rhinebeck, N.Y., and was decapitated in an effort to exorcise Satan. The most peculiar aspect of this violence is the suddenness with which it erupts and then disappears, as though a switch is pulled and cult members react automatically.

Apart from reported cases of cult members attacking outsiders, there have been some bizarre occurrences when violence originally directed against others spilled over and cult members began to attack each other.* This violence may well be the consequence of the suggestibility that is sustained when the brain operates at diminished capacity. Unable to fully assess or integrate information, people in this state tend to become gullible, willing to accept the beliefs of others and to obey their directives. The term *brainwashing* sounds melodramatic. But in light of the mass suicides in Jonestown, perhaps the term is an understatement.

---

* Deprogrammer Galen Kelly tells of being attacked by twenty-five or more Moonies, who, after subduing Kelly and his companion, began blindly beating each other. When the police broke up the melee and the Moonies told them that they had been resisting Kelly's attempt to kidnap them, the police were understandably perplexed.

8 ≡

GETTING OUT

It's a strange thing. The longer I'm out of the cult the less I remember of what I learned in the cult. The lessons I want to take away from being in it I don't want to be simply, "I was glad I was in and now I'm happy I'm out." And I don't want it to be, "Look, I realize I can be fooled and I don't want to be fooled again." It's the cognizance of realizing what one sometimes has to sacrifice, what one is willing to sacrifice, to do what they really want to do.

In fact, that's probably the greatest reason right now I won't, absolutely won't have a relationship with any woman right now of any serious nature. Because I know it's going to take too much effort on my part, and I'm not willing to make that effort right now. Because I made so much effort before, for my last love, and got shattered in a million pieces, because it was all just glass.

—Ex-cult member

Getting permission to visit her parents for Christmas took Alison Peters over a month. During that time she was given literature to read about deprogramming—horrific accounts of torture, of being drugged and put in a mental institution. She was coached about how to behave with her parents: "Soak 'em for all you can get." She arrived home on Christmas Day. The following day, her parents took her shopping for a present.

When they returned home, her brother was waiting with a stranger. Alison didn't think too much of it; she thought the man might be a friend of her parents, until he gave her the special handshake of her cult and remarked upon the necklace she was wearing, "You're a member of the Children of God."

"When he said all that, I knew immediately who he was, and I had this rush through my body. First I thought, 'This is my ultimate test for God. I'm either going to die or I'm going to be used on this earth in a very special way, for I'm face to face with the Devil in the flesh.' "

Alison had just met Ted Patrick. Patrick, "Black Lightning," as he is sometimes called, was the first of the deprogrammers, and the most controversial. He began his crusade against cults in the early 1970s, after his own son was nearly converted to the Children of God. Patrick investigated the group, and what he found propelled him into action. In consequence, he has been jailed and continually involved in court cases, and his methods have been attacked both by the cults and by those who oppose them. Nonetheless, he continues his campaign against what he considers to be an unmitigated evil.

Alison: "My mother and father and my brother and Ted were there in the kitchen, and my initial reaction was to get out of there physically, but there was no way I could do it. The next idea was to do as I had been told—to keep chanting, praying inside, staying in the Kingdom of God—and wait until there was a moment of lax in their security and then make a run for it, conning them in the meantime if necessary. If worse came to worse and there was no escape, it meant God wanted to use me in Heaven. He didn't want to use me on earth. And it would be much better to do that [to commit suicide] than give up the Kingdom of God."

Most cult members who are forcibly deprogrammed react

much as Alison did. Trapped, confronted by the "Devil," they initially want desperately to escape. Deprogrammers expect this. They also expect that their clients will begin to chant and meditate in order to escape internally.

"The cults," Patrick maintains, "completely destroy the mind. They destroy your ability to question things, and in destroying your ability to think, they also destroy your ability to feel. You have no desires, no emotions, you feel no pain, no joy, no nothing.

"When you deprogram people, you force them to think. The only thing I do is shoot them challenging questions. I hit them with things that they haven't been programmed to respond to. I keep them off balance, and this forces them to begin questioning, to open their minds."[1] But if he deems it necessary, Patrick also uses tactics to shock his clients into reacting. He has torn up photographs of the individual's cult leader and cut off the ritual ponytail of Hare Krishna members.[2]

Alison: "First I said to my father, 'What are you going to do, put me in an insane asylum?' And he said, 'No, we just want to talk to you; this man just wants to talk to you.' And Ted looked right at me and said, 'Moses David's [leader of the Children of God] real name is David Berg. He's a criminal. If I ever see that motherfucking sonofabitch, I'll kill him.' And I thought, 'Oh my God, this man is the Devil!'" She threw up her hands and rushed out of the room shouting that she'd rather kill herself than listen to Patrick. Her family tried to reason with her, to no avail. "Why are you trying to take away the only happiness I've ever found?" she screamed.

Alison's deprogramming was relatively short and easy. Within twenty minutes of her confrontation with Patrick, she felt herself starting to cry. She'd begin to cry and try to hold it back. When her mother walked over to her, weeping, Alison could no longer restrain her tears. "I remember I just looked at her and started to cry, and she came over and just hugged me, and I remember I pulled away from her, and then I said to myself, 'Okay, that's it. I believe there's a God, and if this is real, God, you're going to show me, and if it isn't, I have faith you're going to get me out of it.' "

Reluctantly, she agreed to talk with Patrick, though she continued to fear he might be the Devil. There was, as she expressed it, an internal struggle going on. Some of what Patrick said would penetrate for a moment or two, and then her mind would cloud over again. "All of a sudden I became very silent, and I began to think to myself, 'My God, he may be right, and I may not have to do all these things [for the cult] that I hate so much.' After that realization, everything changed. I looked up and I noticed the bookcases, my father's and mother's and brother's faces. The room solidified, came into focus. There was an actual visual change, and that was so overwhelming and so profound that I was speechless. I looked up and said, 'Wow!' "

Such an experience during deprogramming, according to Ted Patrick, is not the exception but the rule. "The first time I lay eyes on a person I can tell if his mind is working or not. Then as I begin to question him, I can determine exactly how he has been programmed. From then on, it's all a matter of language. It's talking and knowing what to talk about. I start challenging every statement the person makes. I start moving his mind, slowly, pushing it with questions, and I watch every move that mind makes. I know everything it is going to do, and when I hit on that one certain point that strikes home, I push it. I stay with that question—whether it's about God, the devil, or that person's having rejected his parent. I keep pushing and pushing. Then there'll be a minute, a second, when the mind snaps, when the person realizes he's been lied to by the cult and he just snaps out of it. It's like turning on the light in a dark room. They're in an almost unconscious state of mind, and then I switch the mind from unconsciousness to consciousness, and it snaps, just like that. It's like seeing a person change from a werewolf into a man. It's a beautiful thing, the personality changes, the eyes, the voice. Where they had hate and a blank expression, you can see feeling again." [3]

Alison's deprogramming was not over. In fact, the hardest part was yet to come. What had occurred had taken only a few hours. Like her original conversion, her deprogramming was a "snapping" experience, a moment of dissociation in which there was a sudden break with existing reality.

After Alison's breaking moment, she, her family, and Ted Patrick continued talking. She was still disoriented. She did not fully trust Patrick, and her mind would switch back to what she had heard about him while in the cult. She began to "float."

Patrick had warned Alison and her parents about floating. He told her to expect that she would float from time to time, that she would feel she'd made a mistake and would want to go back to the group. She'd start picking up her old habits of chanting and praying. When that happens, he advised, do something, anything to get your mind off it. Hum a song, talk to your parents, but get your mind off it.

"After this rush of feelings," Alison said, "the overriding feeling became fear. I felt like a child again in a lot of ways, that I had this void, that I was sick and needed to be taken care of and protected. The idea that something could be so powerful to take my mind that way was incredibly frightening."

At the suggestion of Patrick, Alison slept with her parents that night. While she slept, the struggle she had faced during the day was reenacted. She dreamed of being torn between her parents and the cult. In her dream, she was back with the group, having been deceived by the deprogramming and guilty of listening to the Devil. She awoke in a terrible panic, and realized that she had been chanting, or "praising" in her sleep. "That's something we used to do a lot. We were told that Jesus is watching over you every little minute, and when you wake up in the middle of the night and roll over, that's his way of letting you know he's watching over you. Therefore you should thank him and praise him even while you sleep."

Ted Patrick left the next day and was replaced by an ex-cult member who was to take over Alison's "rehabilitation." Jennifer would be Alison's constant companion for the next two weeks, most of which would be spent at Jennifer's parents' home. The only rule in the rehabilitation was that Alison be responsible for all decisions. Each morning she would decide how they would spend the day.

The day of Jennifer's arrival, she and Alison went shopping, as Alison had left the cult with only the clothes on her back. It was her first, painful lesson in decision making. "It took me two hours to decide on one blouse. It had no meaning. I would look at the blouse and would think, 'Is this something that I really like?' And then it would just fade away. I only managed to buy one shirt that day, and I was exhausted by the end of it."

Most of the two weeks spent with Jennifer, though difficult, was a period of tremendous excitement and rediscovery. "I almost felt like I was going through my adolescence in fast pace all over again." She had to relearn how to talk to people, how to relate to her peers, and to sort out her own feelings about sexuality. The hardest time for her was when she was in the shower alone. Then she would panic: "I'd be so frightened, I'd try to sing, and I couldn't even remember the songs."

Coming home was a letdown. She became depressed and confused. She began doubting everything, questioning herself, the meaning of life, and wondering what to do with herself, how to explain to her friends what had happened. Her feelings of loss were compounded by shame and guilt. "I felt ashamed that I as a person, Alison Peters, would do something this stupid. Ed used to try to get me into this group three years ago, and here, before I had even realized it, I was—*zip*—right into it. Sold, one hundred percent sold."

Alison's depression lasted a month. Then she received a call from Patrick asking her if she was interested in helping him out with deprogrammings. It was a solution. Alison worked for Patrick for six months, and when she returned home this time, the worst of her ordeal was over.

Getting out of a cult is never easy. Many people do not leave without outside help, although a surprisingly large proportion, about one-third, do manage to walk out on their own.* Why one person stays and another defects is hard to pinpoint. Researchers have noted that, apart from purely idiosyncratic factors in the cult members' personalities, there are several weak points in the conversion process that may account for voluntary attrition. Fatigue and boredom with tedious work is one reason. The initial drama of being involved in a messianic struggle gives way to the mundaneness of day-to-day chores. The convert, at

---

* Marc Galanter, one of the few researchers who have administered psychological questionnaires with the full cooperation of cult personnel, reports in a 1978 study of a Southern California branch of the Unification Church that of the 104 persons attending the initial "Two-Day Workshop," only 29 percent remained to continue in the next sequence, the "Seven-Day Workshop." Thereafter, the dropout percentages diminished. Of the 29 percent continuing, 12 percent dropped out after seven days, and 17 percent continued on into the "Twenty-one-Day Workshop." After that workshop, 9 percent joined the Church (8 percent dropped out) and of those, 6 percent remained as members four months later. Early dropouts, according to Galanter, had "weaker affiliative ties toward the group and less acceptance of its religious beliefs" than those who stayed. The later dropouts had strong outside ties.[4]

On the other hand, psychologist Margaret Thaler Singer, who has counseled many

first made to feel loved and important, becomes another cog in the organization. Some people become disillusioned by this monotony and leave the group, and others become so exhausted they are unable to continue. They leave, feeling like failures. Another weak point in the conversion process is the continuing contact cult members have with the outside world. By the very acts of selling goods or soliciting for the cult, members are exposed to information that may shake their commitment. An article in a newspaper, a letter from home, or a memory stirred by a song or a familiar neighborhood can contribute to a decision to leave the cult.* Strong attachments to people outside the group can pull them away as well.

The amount of time spent in a cult is also a critical element in the decision to leave. As would be expected, the longer one stays, the harder it becomes to leave. Length of stay is related to another important consideration, position in the cult hierarchy: the more one has invested in a group, the more difficult and less attractive it becomes to leave.

Most people, however, even those who feel dissatisfied with the cult and hope for rescue, are unable to leave. The very consideration of "defection" produces conflicting feelings of guilt and fear. Loath to betray their friends, they are at the same time terrified at the thought of the cult's retaliation. Nor is the prospect of the outside world undaunting. Having rejected that

---

ex-cult members, reports that out of approximately 100 treated, 75 percent needed outside help in getting out of their respective cults.[5] And in a survey of 400 cult members, researchers Conway and Siegelman report that 71 percent were deprogrammed.[6] The discrepancies between Galanter and the others possibly stems from their sources. Singer's and Conway and Siegelman's information comes from ex-members, while Galanter has studied cult members. His figures, interestingly, reflect poorly on the success rate of, in this case, the Unification Church.

* Researchers also cite "incomplete suppression" of undesired thoughts and tendencies as another factor in voluntary attrition, as well as "habituation," the tendency of many of the pleasures of the group to lose their appeal over time.[7]

world, cult members are unsure of their ability to manage in it once again.

Once they have left, whether voluntarily or involuntarily, ex-cult members are hardly over their problems. Most feel lost and disoriented. Between two worlds, they commonly experience the sensation of floating, or being unable to stay grounded in the here and now. One young man, much to his terror, would suddenly hear his cult leader's voice saying, "You'll always come back. You are with us. You can never separate." [8] Hearing this disembodied voice, he would forget where he was and what he was doing.

Ex-members are also extremely suggestible, perceiving the simple remarks of their friends and acquaintances as commands to be obeyed. Indecision plagues them. They have difficulty making even simple decisions and feel overwhelmed by the sheer magnitude of their options. Used to following orders and to having the day's activities totally planned, one young woman found herself unable to keep a job or look after her apartment. "I come in and can't decide whether to clean the place, make the bed, cook, or sleep, or what. I just can't decide about anything, and I sleep instead. I don't even know what to cook. The group used to reward me with candy and sugar when I was good. Now I'm ruining my teeth by just eating candy bars and cake." [9]

In one of the few large-scale surveys of cult members, researchers Flo Conway and Jim Siegelman noted that after leaving their cults the majority of their four hundred respondents reported they had experienced serious mental, emotional, and physical disturbances while in the cults. Physiological problems included extreme weight gain or loss, abnormal skin conditions, menstrual abnormalities, higher-pitched voices, and reduced facial hair growth among men. Among the mental and emotional effects of cult life were feelings of guilt, fear, hostility, and depression, violent outbursts, and suicidal tendencies. More than half of the respondents also reported experiencing disturbances of perception, memory, and cognition.[10] According to this survey, full rehabilitation took an average of sixteen months and was noticeably swifter and less traumatic among those who were deprogrammed.[11]

The problems of getting out of a cult and readjusting to the world outside take time to resolve. As a result, a market has arisen for deprogrammers, halfway houses, and psychologists specializing in cults.

Ted Patrick is one of the pioneers in this field. His authoritarian approach, however, has been widely criticized, for in many ways his deprogrammings seem to be another form of conversion, a brainwashing in reverse. Though acknowledging the similarities, he defends his methods on grounds of motivation. Unlike the cults' objective, he maintains, his purpose is to get a person thinking and functioning independently again. He has also been criticized for setting himself up as a personal halfway house. Ex-cult members frequently come to live with his family and work with him in other deprogrammings, as did Alison. This too smacks of cult tactics—having new converts recruit others as part of their own conversion process. And while the use of ex-members in deprogramming is widespread, Patrick's relationship with them is intense. It is this aspect that has come under fire.

Galen Kelly, another well-known deprogrammer, is one of the critics. He does not believe that the "snapping" variety of deprogramming is effective over time. "It's an unstable reconversion, though it's a quick and easy way of doing it." He recalls the time one deprogrammer snapped a person out of her "cult mind," walked over to her parents, and smugly announced, "You'll be glad to know your daughter's a Christian again." "But," responded the somewhat dazed parents, for it had all occurred so quickly, "she used to be Jewish."

"In the emotionally charged deprogramming designed to elicit a snapping reaction," Kelly says, "people are told things like: 'Look at yourself in the mirror, this is a picture of you graduating from high school. Look at what you are now.' 'Look at what you're doing to your mother.' [The mother is hysterical in a corner.] And they snap out in a very emotionally charged encounter. But then, days later, you get into this floating syndrome. They think, 'Well, maybe Moon *is* the Messiah, and why did I elect to leave? Because my mother was crying in the corner?' And they don't really know. You can psychologically manipulate and snap individuals out, but when they sit back and reevaluate, especially in the periods of depression that follow, they wonder, 'Why did I leave? There was a great deal of yelling and screaming and gnashing of teeth and wringing of hands, but why did I really leave?' "

In fact, deprogrammings are not always successful. Some people undergo it only to turn around and return to the cult. Some of the unsuccessful deprogrammings have resulted in lawsuits directed against parents and deprogrammers by cults on behalf of their members.*

Kelly believes that the approach he and his associates have developed works, precisely because it provides the individual with the answer to the question Why did I really leave? "We

---

* *The Advisor*, a newsletter concerned with cult issues, ran a questionnaire for parents regarding deprogramming. The responses were sporadic and thus not statistically significant, though they are interesting. To the question "Was your child ever forcibly deprogrammed?" nineteen responses were received from parents with children in the Unification Church; fifteen answered yes. To the question "If yes, how many failed, how many returned to the cult?" eight failures were reported. One lawsuit was brought against parents and/or deprogrammers, and four children still remained in the cult at the time the questionnaire was published. Five parents of Hare Krishna members reported

don't snap the person out; he evolves out and is educated during that time. He learns why he was more susceptible than other people; how he was converted; how that conversion was maintained; and very importantly, why he left. He also has the confidence that he can make it in the outside world."

Kelly became involved in deprogramming in 1975. Trained as a policeman, he went into retail security, white-collar crime, and then, quite naturally, private investigation, where he first came into contact with distraught parents of cult members. Since then, Kelly has deprogrammed over one hundred fifty clients, most of whom had been members of the Unification Church.

"Portal to portal," as Kelly puts it, his deprogramming is a fifteen-day "operation." First, you have to "effect custody." Then a five-person team—two family members, Kelly, and two associates, one of whom is usually an ex-cult member from the same cult as the client—holes up together in a motel with the cult member.

"The first phase, almost to the clock, takes three days. In the first three days, I hope to overcome the initial hostility and fear on the part of the subject, elicit his cooperation and rapport, and start to impart factual information of three areas: the science of mind control, the general controversy surrounding his group and the cult phenomenon in general, and theology."

Mind control gets top billing. "You lay out a case from the textbooks for support, that mind control is real, powerful, sub-

---

that three had been forcibly deprogrammed, with two successes and one failure. Three children remained in the cult. Three Scientologists had been forcibly deprogrammed, with two successes and one failure. And, out of six responses from parents of children in Divine Light Mission, all six had been deprogrammed, three of those once, two twice, and one three times. Five of the six were out of the group, while one remained in.[12]

Deprogramming is not only risky, it is expensive, with costs frequently running in excess of $10,000 to cover the expenses of deprogrammers, detectives, security, lodging, travel, and legal and mental-health consultants.

tle, self-generating, the product of good treatment, not abusive treatment, requiring voluntary participation on the part of the subject or 'victim,' and the fact that it doesn't produce a mindless zombie, but a thinking, logical person whose frame of reference is a little off."

This discussion serves two immediate purposes. It confirms to the ex-cult member that what he has undergone is real and powerful while reassuring him that he is not crazy. According to Kelly, it also accomplishes several other aims. It explains the nature of the conversion experience in abstract terms; it points out that conversion requires the suspension of individual judgment, while deprogramming asks the person to examine all the evidence and make up his own mind; and it conveys factual information while simultaneously serving as a mental exercise to get the person thinking again.

"When they start to understand the things I outlined about mind control and can begin to relate it to their own experience, then a serious chink has been taken out of their unquestioned loyalty to the group."

The discussion of actual cult practices is also very important. Debunking, however, must be backed up by tangible evidence. The deprogrammer must be able to document his charges against the cult.

Theology is the most difficult and amorphous subject of discussion. "We do tell them, 'You have the right to believe anything you want to. You want to believe Moon is the Messiah, fine. But we have to distinguish freedom of belief from freedom of action on belief. Bribing congressmen in the name of the Messiah is against the law of the land and the public mores.'"

At the end of the three days, Kelly, his team, and his client are ready to leave the motel and move the operation to New York, Kelly's base. In the second phase of the deprogramming, the client is taken to visit experts in the field, primarily psychiatrists and theologians. The psychiatrists perform two functions: they explain the nature of the mind control and psychological manipulation used by cults to the client, while simultaneously evaluating him and the progress of his deprogramming. The theologians (from the three major faiths) help reveal the flaws in cult teachings and the discrepancies between the cult theology and the theologies of the Old and New Testaments from which cult theologies claim to derive. They also reaffirm to the individual that the spiritual quest is not in vain—that there is a God and there is a meaning to life.

During the second phase, the initial team of five is gradually pared down. By its end, usually about ten days later, the client is accompanied by only one or two others.

In the final phase of Kelly's program, the person returns home with a member of the staff, who remains for a day or two to help smooth the difficulty of returning to the family.

Full reintegration into society requires much more time. By the end of the fifteen-day operation, however, Kelly feels that the real battle is over.* He does recognize that some of his clients will need additional help. Many, in fact, decide to undertake psychological counseling, often with one of the psychiatrists visited during deprogramming. Kelly opposes halfway houses, though, because he feels that they are themselves too cultlike. "You've got six or seven or twenty recent ex-cult

---

* Kelly estimates that his overall success rate is 85 percent. The failures are the result of several factors: "operational screw-ups, when for instance cult members suddenly arrive at the scene; bad family dynamics; a realization on the part of the person being deprogrammed that he or she will not be able to achieve as much outside the cult as inside it—this is often a factor among people with high-level positions in the cult; and finally, very serious psychological problems in the person being deprogrammed which may even have existed prior to cult involvement." Although Kelly, as he puts it, "does not want to abdicate responsibility" for his failures, he believes that most of them fall into these categories.

members all living together in a communal environment under a central figure. It becomes as difficult to leave that halfway house as it was to leave the cult." He warns against group counseling for much the same reasons, citing the experience of Dr. Hardat Sukhdeo, a Newark-based psychiatrist with whom he works. "Dr. Sukhdeo ran counseling sessions for the survivors of the People's Temple. And a strange and interesting thing began to develop. They were having mini–People's Temple meetings. They got together thinking of People's Temple and looking forward to the next People's Temple meeting. People started getting very suicidal. It was the People's Temple all over again."

When I talked with Dr. Sukhdeo, he confirmed this. "The Jonestown people only wanted to talk about Jonestown. It was their world that was destroyed, and all the content of their thoughts was Jonestown. Each time they'd say, 'Okay, this time we're not going to talk about it, because it makes us sad,' and then they'd go ahead and do it anyway."

Dr. Sukhdeo believes one of the main problems in treating ex-cult members, which deprogramming does not fully address, is that when you take someone out of a cult, you remove a support system, often without having anything to take its place. Before he agrees to take on a patient, he conducts interviews with the patient's family: "If I find out that maybe from age fourteen, the family was not a support system to this child, and at age twenty-eight, the person is in a cult and the parent is saying, 'Let's get him out,' my question is, 'If you take him out, what are you going to do with him? You haven't been a support system for the child for so many years.' Many times the answer is that it's best to leave him there."

To illustrate this dilemma, he mentions one of the Jonestown survivors, a young black man who was one of the few who escaped through the jungle: "Jones had rescued this boy from reform school. He was a bad boy, he had done everything bad. Jones took him out, took him to California, gave him clothes, a home, a job, a place in the community. Sure he controlled him, but compared to what he had before, it was worth it." This survivor had not wanted to return to the States. He hoped to stay in Guyana, and his only regret was that the utopia had failed.

Dr. Sukhdeo has no special program for treating ex-cult members, but believes his success with them can be attributed to his special sensitivity to their problems. He sympathizes with their idealism and alienation, ascribing the tremendous rise in cults to the deterioration of our social institutions, the family in particular. In his view, the common denominator in cult membership is alienation; the personal crisis that precipitates joining is simply the straw that broke the camel's back. "When I look around at our institutions—the family, the churches, the colleges—and the children tell me they're all fakes, they're right—they are. Our institutions are failing our young people, and so are our values. When they look at their parents, who have money but who are not happy, who are physically together but not emotionally together, they ask, 'What do I want that for?' I think that if you really look at the questions that the people in cults ask, there's a lot to it."

Psychiatrist John Clark, who knows of Galen Kelly's work, has a different approach. He believes that ordinary psychotherapy, however sensitive, is not enough. The cult experience produces special problems that must be confronted directly. Clark and his associates have devised a plan of therapy that combines standard psychotherapeutic techniques with an understanding of the biological functioning of the brain.

The main problem with people who have recently come out

of a cult, Clark says, whether through deprogramming or some spontaneous act, is that they experience a difficulty in the flow of consciousness. Normally, the central nervous system is "continuously reacting and adapting to stress. Because the system is so complex and the information it must evaluate so varied and changing, there is in the mind's life a continuous process of evaluation and readjustment to the infinite possibilities of adaptation. The process of cult conversion, which skillfully manipulates group dynamics, employs excessive stress to break down the mind's ability to carry out this complex human process and, in the end, substitutes a rigid and dull simplicity in which the adaptive function, at least in its higher intellectual forms, has atrophied."

When people come out of cults, their consciousness is very empty or filled with hallucinative phenomena. The ordinary mental flow has been disrupted. Instead, there is a lessening of thoughts, or a great increase in the flow of thoughts, or an interruption of the flow of thought with bizarre and highly charged or more vivid thoughts. This sets up a tendency toward dissociation, toward an emergency state of the central nervous system, and results as well in an inability to handle the normal tasks of a well-functioning mind. People coming out of cults, Clark maintains, can't think as well, can't make decisions as well, and can't act as well.

The first step in Dr. Clark's therapy is standard psychiatric procedure. He tries to discover as much about the patient as possible. In the case of ex-cult members, he tries to find out about the patient's relationships before conversion, to discover what kind of a mind and what kind of a life the individual had. This information gives him a starting point for his talk with the client.

The next step, however, deviates from traditional psychological counseling. Rather than wait for the patient to talk, to produce information, the therapist must assume the responsibility for producing mental content. "If someone is listening to someone else talk," Dr. Clark explains, "that tends to be the center of the process of consciousness. With cult members, whose flow of consciousness is altered, where the mind is either empty or overloaded, it is the responsibility of the therapist to fill that void by conversation, by information, and by all kinds of social actions. This is true even when the mind is overloaded. Then the therapist must compete with the overload. It's necessary for the therapist to talk, to be conversational, interesting, humorous—somebody worth listening to and worth identifying with."

It is also necessary, he maintains, to talk about the cult experience as much as possible. It is important that it not be blotted out as shameful. The therapist must talk about the positive aspects of the cult as well as the negative. For the individual to be able to fully integrate the two worlds, he must be able to recognize what was valuable about the experience as well as to tolerate what was terrible. "You've got to do what is necessary to get anybody over what is a serious psychological trauma in order then to avoid the deeper split in consciousness. That way the cult experience becomes real, not magical, maybe not pleasant to think about, but maybe before long it becomes humorous, kind of silly, a little shameful, and then, in a way, a general experience to be applied to a lot of other life problems. This can be done, but it has to start out with a conversational, open, available therapist who's not afraid to talk."

Shame is one of the invariable consequences of cult involvement. Like Alison, most ex-members feel "stupid" for having been taken in, ashamed of the fact that they were "duped," and ashamed of the humiliation to which they allowed themselves to be subjected and to which they subjected others.

Moreover, explaining to someone unfamiliar with the cults just why one joined is neither simple nor straightforward. "People just can't understand what the group puts into your mind," one of psychologist Margaret Singer's patients told her. "How they play upon your guilts and needs. Psychological pressure is much heavier than a locked door. You can bust a locked door in terror or anger, but chains that are mental are hard to break. The heaviest thing I've ever done is leaving the group, breaking those real heavy bonds on my mind." [13]

Ex-cult members also feel ashamed of having brought others into the cult and of the things they did in the name of the cult. "You lose your sense of right and wrong," one person told me. "You lose your gut feelings. You're given directions and you follow them."

"What you've got to do," Dr. Clark explained, "is take away the shame as quickly as possible without taking away the responsibility." In order to accomplish this, he feels it is very helpful to explain to the patient in theoretical terms something of what has happened to him or her. A theoretical framework for understanding the experience allows the patient to translate what is frightening and incomprehensible into manageable terms. As Dr. Clark puts it, "If you give an individual who is in the process of developing amnesia of a past trauma a matrix of theory for it, the memory will stick to the matrix and won't go away." Moreover, the act of translating is a distancing process and helps eliminate some of the shame. People stop feeling, "I have done something terrible" and "I was an idiot," and can begin to understand that what happened to them was a supremely human experience.

Another critical step in the therapy is to try to reunite the individual with his past. It is necessary, Dr. Clark maintains, to deal with old loves and old hurts in the family and in other relationships so the person understands the forces working on him at the time he got into difficulty and joined the cult. "The therapist must try to validate the past, to affirm that, 'Yes, you did go through high school, you did have parents and siblings, and you were making choices and progress.'"

The question of reestablishing an identity that encompasses both the cult experience and the past is especially difficult, as cult members have been trained to block out their pasts. One person who had not yet left his cult described to me his sensation of disorientation when he returned home for a visit: "I went to all these places where I used to live and saw people I used to know and was just socked with all these remembrances and all these weird feelings about what I was doing and their attitude toward me—some people thinking I was in a cult and other people thinking I was the old person they knew from college. I remember especially being in my parents' home and, for reasons unknown to me, I went through the entire house. I just started looking through the house, through drawers and cupboards and cabinets and through all the pictures. I wasn't looking for anything, I was just looking."

The individual coming out of a cult is fragmented. It is important for the therapist to validate all the different parts of the fragmented self in order to facilitate integration. The ex-member has to accept the reality of his experience in the cult as well as the reality of his life before he joined. "It's necessary," John Clark believes, "to make sure they recognize they've not come back into a perfect world—that they're right back where they were, a little older, but more experienced. And it's necessary for them also to know the degree of damage that they must face so they don't come out of the treatment feeling they're better off than they were. They have to know how long it's going to take to get well. They have to be told it's going to take a year before they can really feel as though their heads will stay up all by themselves. That they've stepped back a couple of years, that if they're going to go ahead, they'll be with people who are younger. They've lost two or three years. They've lost relationships, and they need to be told that they'll have trouble with very close relationships, that they're going to have to take chances and be rebuffed and have difficulties, but they'll make it somehow or other. You've got to warn them, to be a little bit magical, to be wise."

Ex-cult members also experience a problem of loss and real depression. A person who comes out of a cult has been plunged into a grief state. He has lost something, and it can't be returned. There is, Clark acknowledges, a tendency to float back toward the lost cult experience, into the other personality that is lost. These feelings must be dealt with by the therapist as though he were dealing with the real elements of grief. There is a real loss. Something has died. The person cannot go back. He has a right to grieve and mourn.

In the course of the therapy, Dr. Clark often assigns a task to the patient as he leaves the office after a session. The task will concern an issue that has come up that day, an emotional jam of one sort or another. "If, for example, someone is having trouble with choices, then instead of telling the person to stop having trouble making choices, it is a good idea to set up a fairly concrete process of choice making. Give him a real problem, but always tell him exactly why you are doing it: 'This is a way of not just playing with your mind, but stressing it in a way where you become responsible to me. You focus on it because I asked you to. It's a way of getting the flow of consciousness started by the process of suggestion.' It's not quite the same as hypnosis, but it's not that different either. The difference is that I would not be pushing the individual toward trance state, but toward increased consciousness."

The final element in Dr. Clark's plan is the "usual thing that goes on in all good therapy. The therapist has got to care. He's got to share in the outrage and not be separated from it. To value the negative side as well as the positive side of the whole experience. To laugh and almost to cry at the losses, the hurts, the guilts. To help the person understand that the people who are still in the cults are really being hurt, but that the individual's guilt about it is something that will just have to be lived with, but it ought not to kill the person."

Coming out of a cult is a difficult and protracted process. It varies, naturally, from person to person and from cult to cult. It has been reported, for example, that it takes almost twice the time (twenty-six months) for former Scientologists to feel fully rehabilitated as it does the members of other groups. The "Christian" cults—The Way International, the Christ Family, the Tony and Susan Alamo Christian Foundation, and the Church of Bible Understanding, for instance—rated next in average rehabilitation time and in the duration of long-term effects. The amount of time needed for rehabilitation seems to correspond directly to the amount of time spent in intensive ritual and indoctrination exercises.[14]

There are other differences. Strong family ties and a reliable support system help the individual who is trying to leave a cult. Psychological counseling is often highly effective in promoting reintegration. The seriousness of problems that await ex-members is another variable in the reentry process, as is the position held within a cult hierarchy. Those high up have more to lose by defecting and have enjoyed more of the tangible rewards of cult life. It has been observed, too, that people belonging to cults that use rapid conversion techniques often can be "snapped out" with relative ease, while with cults that employ a gradual conversion, getting out is also gradual. I suspect that the cults that allow the individual to integrate his past life with his cult life are more insidious, although it is precisely among these groups where there is greatest evidence of natural attrition.

Notwithstanding these variations, it remains true that getting out, staying out, and reintegrating into the larger society is a drawn-out ordeal. Most psychiatrists and deprogrammers agree that the getting-out process takes between six and eighteen months. Even then, however, the scars are not completely gone. Intimate relationships remain elusive, years have been lost, and the stigma of having belonged to a cult does not easily fade. Cult members have learned a lesson about the human condition that most of us, fortunately, are spared.

9 ≡

CONCLUSION

ults raise fundamental questions about the assumptions on
which our society is based, about the autonomy of the
individual, the relationship between the individual and the community, and the relationship between church and state. The
current cult phenomenon has provoked debate about the ade-
quacy of the Bill of Rights and about the role government
should play in the affairs of its citizens.

There are no hard-and-fast answers to these questions. On
the one hand, the abuses practiced by certain cults are deplora-
ble. Their exploitation of individuals is sad and repellent; their
cavalier attitude toward the laws of this country is outrageous.
No group or person is above the law, and freedom of belief,
however sacred, does not grant freedom of action.

On the other hand, although strange and sometimes sinister
organizations—some of which may not be bona fide religions at
all—claim First Amendment protections, the effort to prevent
them from claiming these protections is often misguided. The
accepted definition of religion is broad enough to encompass all
sorts and species of groups, and freedom of belief is not really
the issue. The real question arises from the conflict between the
freedoms granted to religious groups and other freedoms guaranteed by the Bill of Rights.

The cult question, far from being simple or straightforward, is a conundrum, filled with gray areas, contradictions, and emotional obstacles. For example, the whole discussion of brainwashing, which is pivotal to an assessment of cults, is emotionally charged.

Moreover, cults are not a unique or bizarre phenomenon. They are born out of a certain social context, and they are part of it. In many ways, cults are not unlike many popular therapies available today. They also share characteristics with the current evangelical revival. Not only are the lines that separate cults from groups we more readily accept often very fine, but there are also many varieties and gradations among the cults.

When we ask what should be done about the cults, we are of necessity addressing a larger set of issues. Ultimately, though, the answer is simple. For as long as we live in a society where we believe it is important to allow groups like the Nazi party to exist (so long as they don't violate the law), we must tolerate the cults. They are one of the costs of democracy.

Haphazard though it is, the evidence gathered from journalists, psychiatrists, ex-members, parents' groups, sociological surveys, and the cults themselves suggests that there are more cults today than ever before. They are also wealthier, more influential, and more sophisticated than cults of the past. Any assessment of today's cults, however, must determine just how different they are from their predecessors.

The salient characteristics of cults have remained constant throughout history. To recap briefly, they are groups that hold themselves apart in some way from the rest of the world; they are by nature antagonistic toward society, their members bound by a fervent ideology and belief in a spiritual leader. The classic structure of messianic cults is authoritarian; followers, subjugated to an all-powerful leader or hierarchy of leaders, are dependent and submissive, believing that their salvation is contingent on abject obedience.

Yet while the basic features of cults are unchanging, their specific characteristics reflect the particular time, place, and culture in which they arise. Similarly, whether a cult is destructive to its followers or constructive is a separate judgment that can be made only after evaluating the specific features of a given cult. The current cults in this country, then, are at once part of a general class of phenomena that is hardly new at all, and, at the same time, they are unique.

One characteristic that distinguishes today's cults is the techniques they use to produce and maintain conversion. Many have combined the techniques that produce traditional religious ecstatic experience (talking in tongues, trance states), the confrontational therapeutic practices derived from the human-potential movement (encounter groups and psychodrama), and the tactics of high-powered salesmanship. This combination, in itself, is not all that unusual. The hellfire-and-brimstone revival preachers of the 1800s also used a combination of rhythmic music, prayer, fear, guilt, and personal confrontation to facilitate conversion. The difference is that the current cults have learned how to prolong the dissociated states produced by these tactics, so that rather than representing transitory moments of spiritual transcendence (as in the past), such states have become a habituated mode of behavior. The difference is one of degree. The intensity and prolongation of these techniques, then, constitute a dramatic departure, making possible a degree of control over members that earlier cults could not claim.

The result of this prolongation is an alteration in the functioning of the central nervous system. The brain adapts to the dissociated state if it is sufficiently protracted, and this adaptation produces a chain reaction affecting the brain function, the hormonal system, and, ultimately, the behavior or "personality" of the individual. While the precise mechanisms of this chain reaction can be only speculated about, enough is known from a variety of experiments to corroborate that the net effect of isolation from one's usual environment and prolonged dissociation is an alteration in ordinary brain processes. The term *brainwashing* is simply a colloquial description of this effect. It does not necessarily imply robotlike behavior, but rather, dramatically altered behavior. As parents and psychiatrists have observed, cult members are changed from their former selves. Their behavior is typically flat, passive, without humor or vitality. They have difficulty concentrating and are at a loss when asked to make independent judgments or decisions. The degree of change in individuals varies, depending upon the intensity of indoctrination and the degree of isolation to which they have been subjected, as well as on purely personal factors.

One survey of former cult members correlated intellectual and emotional impairment with the amount of time spent in intense ritual activities—chanting, praying, meditating, confessional rituals, and group sermons. As might be expected, members of cults that devoted the most time to these activities—up to seventy hours a week—were most severely affected.

Another distinguishing feature of the contemporary cults is their constituencies. Traditionally, cults have attracted marginal groups in the population, people who, though not necessarily of the lowest social strata, were outside the mainstream of society. American cults have historically drawn their followers from groups that have suffered prejudice, from immigrant groups, and from people whose expectations have been thwarted. They have always attracted marginal individuals or misfits as well.

The followers of the current cults are not only from those

marginal groups. They are predominantly white and middle-class. Most are in their late teens or early twenties and educated, over half having attended college. The population of the therapy cults is somewhat older, but is also solidly mainstream and middle-class. These people stand in marked contrast to the typical followers of cults of the past. To maintain that they too are marginal to the American mainstream requires that a psychological definition of marginality replace what has largely, though not exclusively, been an economic and social definition. In the past, marginality referred to an external rather than an internal state.

The constituency of today's cults reflects a number of related factors. Young people, in the throes of leaving their families and establishing themselves as adults, are particularly vulnerable, and the present cults have targeted these young people for conversion. Above all, the constituency of the cults reflects a general dissatisfaction with the mainstream culture.

One of the lasting results of the war in Vietnam and the ensuing counterculture movement was an undermining of established institutions. In their place, the counterculture movement offered alternatives that ranged from political activism to utopian communes and Eastern mystical religions. The common denominator of these groups was a repudiation of accepted values and, in particular, a rejection of the "materialist" culture.

The recent cults are an outgrowth of the counterculture movement, articulating many of its sentiments. Yet cults are a hybrid. They transform the idealism, the quest for personal realization, and the desire for community into a structure that cannot be more unlike the freewheeling counterculture. The cults are disciplined and authoritarian. They offer a rigid structure and appeal to people who, while sharing many of the dissatisfactions and aspirations of the counterculture movement, cannot cope with the freedoms it has unleashed.

Cults also share characteristics with the American revival movement, with its focus on personal religious experience, devotional prayer, asceticism, intense religious enthusiasm, and an inherent criticism of the religious establishment. Historically, the two forms of religious activity were often connected. Both emerged during periods of social crisis, and both expressed a combination of renewed spiritualism and social dissent. The American revival tradition, in addition, has for the last one hundred years stressed salvation as its primary purpose, employing a slick, businesslike approach to streamline that process.

Since the late 1960s this country has been in the midst of a widespread revitalization movement, an awakening that has assumed different forms and has affected large segments of the population. The counterculture, the fundamentalist revival, cults, and the human-potential movement are all manifestations of this phenomenon, as all deplore the current state of social corruption, and all offer programs that promise personal and social salvation. However disparate they may appear, they all stress the importance of personal conversion, and many employ similar tactics to bring it about.

This perspective provides a context for appraising the current cult phenomenon. Not only are cults themselves part of an established tradition, but they are one of a number of manifestations of a larger movement that is sweeping the country. While an appreciation of this context by no means neutralizes the impact of cults, it does suggest that they are not as unique and untoward as some critics have maintained.

One of the inevitable questions raised by the cults regards their relation to the established churches. While it is historically true that cults have often represented a stage in the evolution of what eventually becomes an established religion, and that with legitimacy some of the extremism of cults drops away, it is also true that the experience of belonging to a cult cannot really be compared to membership in an established religion. For cults do not confine themselves to providing a spiritual dimension to the lives of members. They do not seek to enhance or make palatable the existing social structure. They seek to replace it. And while some of the techniques of the cults resemble those practiced by the established religions, they are used differently and for different purposes. Prayer and meditation in the current cults have become instruments of control and coercion, rather than a source of inner peace and equanimity.

Furthermore, the nature of experience in the religious orders is qualitatively different from that in the cults. For although future nuns and priests, like cult members, are asked to renounce the secular world for a life of sacrifice and asceticism, they are made aware of the kind of life they are entering beforehand, and they are asked to deliberate seriously before taking their vows. This openness stands in marked contrast to the practices of many cults, which deliberately deceive followers about their identity, their purpose, and the nature of the life they ask members to follow. Although not all of the new cults are guilty of such deception (nor are all of the established religions above such manipulative practices), these distinctions generally hold, and they add up to a qualitatively different experience. The efflorescence of cults, instead of replacing the established churches, points up their failure to satisfy the spiritual needs of many people.

The historical relation between cults and religions suggests, however, that the ultimate role of the cults may indirectly be to revitalize the established churches. Most revitalization movements do end up by generating reform, their more extreme components either dying off or being absorbed by the prevailing culture.

Whatever the ultimate role or fate of the cults, there is no doubt that some of them are causing real damage right now. The greatest harm is suffered by individual cult followers. Although some people maintain that they have been helped by their cult experience, many feel they have been financially and emotionally exploited, taken in by a racket that they were too naïve and too indoctrinated to recognize. There is a large store of horror stories about life in the cults—about rape, sexual humiliation, starvation, child abuse, beatings, forced labor, unattended physical illness, and personal degradation.[1] Evidence abounds that these stories—including a growing number of cult-related suicides, deaths, nervous breakdowns, and psychotic episodes—are not mere inventions. Jonestown, of course, provides the single most lurid illustration of the danger of cults, with nine hundred people dead on Jones's orders.

But even for those who manage to leave the cults without permanent damage, the aftermath of their involvement is a prolonged and difficult period. Guilt, anger, shame, depression, impaired mental functioning, periods of disorientation, and fear are its common attributes. For many ex-members, full integration into ordinary society may take years, and frequently is accomplished only with professional psychiatric help.

The other immediate victims of the cults are the families of members. Families are abruptly repudiated and disowned, some harassed or even blackmailed by relatives who have joined cults. The usual reaction of family members is to feel confused, angry, panicked, and, above all, guilty. Feelings of impotence and loss are compounded by social stigma. The parents of cult members in particular are blamed for having lost a child to a cult, and are saddled with the full brunt of the assumption that cults attract only misfits and weirdos. It is psychologically more comfortable for us to perceive cult members and their families as in some way abnormal than to confront our own vulnerability with regard to the cults. Many Americans are unwilling to see that brainwashing techniques exist, are readily available; that even "healthy," "normal" people from "good" homes can, under the right circumstances, be indoctrinated, because indoctrination has as much to do with the biology of the human organism as it does with personal character. We react as though the concept were alien, something we might conceive as happening in China or Iran, but not here at home.

Apart from the individual tragedies, cults present a social danger. The combination of millennial ideology and indoctrination techniques transforms followers into potential little armies whose loyalties belong exclusively to the cults. The inhabitants of Jonestown, for instance, were clearly capable of violence, a violence that was directed outward as well as against themselves. The indoctrination to which they as well as members of other cults were subjected results in an increased suggestibility, dependency, and a willingness to obey orders without reflection. Ex-members have stated that while in their respective cults they were prepared to kill another person, to kill their parents, or to take their own lives if so ordered. And while most cult members have not had to carry out such orders, they are not only prepared, but they have the means to do so. Some cults have even amassed stockpiles of weapons and have trained their followers in their use. At Hare Krishna properties, for example, public officials have discovered a grenade launcher, military-type assault rifles, riot guns, an Ingram submachine gun, pistols, thousands of rounds of ammunition, and the casings, powder, and slugs for fifty thousand more rounds.*

The techniques used by the cults to keep members in line create a propensity for violence, peculiar in the suddenness with which it erupts and then disappears. Add to this inclination an ideology that depicts the cult as God's special army fighting off the Satanic hordes, an egomaniacal leader deluded by power and self-aggrandizement, and the ready availability of arms, and the result is volatile. Some cults have already resorted to violence, or at least have been charged with acts of deception, beatings, extortion, robbery, and psychological violence directed against each other and against outsiders.

The treatment of critics suggests the violent lengths to which some of the cults will go. While Synanon's rattlesnake attack against lawyer Paul Moranz is perhaps the best known of these cases, Scientology's aggressive activities are far more extensive. Scientology maintains a special organization, the Guardian's Office, to deal with critics. The activities of the Guardian's Office have included framing journalist Paulette Cooper by stealing some of her personal stationery and forging bomb-threat letters; compromising the then-mayor of Clearwater, California, Gabriel Cezares, by a phony hit-and-run accident; implicating California Deputy Attorney General Laurance Tapper in a woman's pregnancy; and burglarizing government agencies it felt were interfering with its operations.[3] In 1977, the FBI obtained search warrants and seized twenty-three thousand documents from Scientology headquarters. These docu-

---

* Hare Krishna is not alone. The Way International trains members in weapons use at its college campus at Emporia, Kansas, and its Way Police Force patrols its property at New Knoxville, Ohio. The Divine Light Mission's security force, World Peace Corps, travels with Guru Maharaj Ji in order to protect him. At least two large Unification Church training camps are guarded, and a large arsenal of automatic rifles, shotguns, and handguns were found at Jonestown.[2]

ments were released to the public during the 1979 federal trial of eleven Scientologists who were charged with conspiracy to spy on U.S. agencies, breaking into government offices, stealing government documents, bugging federal agency meetings, and obstructing justice. The seized documents also outlined Scientologists' plans for the infiltration of more than 130 federal agencies, private organizations, and businesses.[4]

A disturbing parallel can be drawn between some of the cults and full-fledged totalitarian states. These groups are ruled by a supreme authority whom no one dares question and who is deemed above the law. Obedience to the leader is valued above all other moral considerations or emotional ties. Indeed, many of the current cults make the renunciation and exploitation of parents a test of loyalty to the group. These groups also share the messianic ideology that characterizes totalitarian states. The world is pictured in black and white. Simple, personalized evil substitutes for the difficult analysis of complex forces and events. All the failures and disappointments in society and in oneself are attributed to an evil group working within both the society and the individual, and thus scapegoats are an essential element in this world view.

In the early days of his national power, when Hitler was asked if he wished the complete destruction of Jews, he replied, "No, it is essential to have a tangible enemy." Anti-Semitism also plays a part in some of the contemporary cults. Reverend Moon tells his followers that the Holocaust was indemnity the Jews paid for having murdered Christ. The Way International recommends reading books like *The Myth of Six Million* and *The Hoax of the Twentieth Century*, which assert that the mass murder of the Jews by the Germans during World War II was a giant hoax perpetrated by "left-wing intellectuals." Cult rhetoric also strikes a familiar, if unhappy, chord. "Why is the

Dollar inflating?" David Berg, founder of the Children of God, asks. "The Jews are selling out their European currencies and buying Dollars instead. . . . Any Christian who stands with the Jews at a time like this is a traitor to his own faith!" [5] The declarations of Lyndon LaRouche, founder of the U.S. Labor party, a political cult, sound as if they could have been written forty years ago: "The U.S. Zionist Lobby, since its creation by Theodor Herzl, Louis Brandeis, Eugene Meyer of Lazard Frères, and the British Foreign Office earlier in this century, has served as a foot-in-the-door for British sabotage of U.S. industrial growth and for the terrorizing of American industrialists and workers." [6]

The anti-Semitism of these groups is not too surprising. Scapegoats, as Hitler pointed out, are necessary to the messianic vision, and Jews have always been preeminent candidates for that role. They are different, relatively few in numbers, and perceived as inordinately powerful. Beyond that, anti-Semitism has a particular meaning for messianic groups because of the biblical designation of Jews as Chosen People, the precise role the cults have claimed for themselves.

Despite the violent nature or potential of some of the cults, there appears to be little chance for them to evolve into an important political force. To do so, they would have to join forces and work together, and any extensive cooperation is not likely, given the egocentric character of cult leaders. The heterogeneity of America also works against the possibility of a coalition of cults arising: the very differences and prejudices in the population militate against any one group gaining a great deal of power.

A realistic projection about the future of the cults must be based on the history of similar groups in this country. Two general fates exist for these movements. They either die away, often upon the death of their leaders, or they become legitimate, fully accepted churches. With legitimization, many of the extreme qualities of these groups fade.

One of the indications of this country's strength is its ability to absorb and assimilate marginal groups. This has been accomplished by informal means as well as through the formal apparatus of the state.

In framing the Constitution, the Founding Fathers were careful to protect the freedom of the individual, establishing boundaries beyond which the state cannot intrude. The freedom of individuals and groups to hold varying beliefs was built into the Constitution, with religious pluralism protected by the First Amendment. As well as protecting the "establishment and free exercise of religion," this amendment implicitly guarantees the individual's freedom of choice. And freedom was thought to belong to the individual rather than to any group to which he might belong. The First Amendment, while protecting religious groups from government interference, was also designed to enable people to make free choices, to freely discuss and examine alternative ideas, and to protect the unrestricted access to information.

In consequence, this country has always been a haven for new and marginal religious groups. Cults, sects, and religious revivals have been a continuing feature of American life. The general attitude toward these groups has been one of resigned acceptance, so long as their practices did not violate social norms. Indeed, alternate belief groups have not encountered antagonism for their beliefs so much as for their habits and customs.

Occasional Supreme Court decisions reveal the shifting balance between personal freedoms protected by the First Amendment and the government's obligation to maintain social order.

Two Supreme Court cases are especially interesting, for they deal, as legal scholar John Richard Burkholder has put it, "not only with the law, but with moral self-understanding of a changing and complex society." [7] The first case arose from the practices of the Mormon church in the late nineteenth century; the second dealt with the I-Am Movement in the 1940s.

The emergence of the Mormon church was part of a religious revival that swept New York State in the mid-nineteenth century. But while some of the groups that appeared at that time were well tolerated by their neighbors, the Mormons' relations with outsiders were strained. Their practice of polygamy was especially controversial.

The first confrontation between the Mormons and the courts occurred in 1878, with the Supreme Court rejecting defendant Reynolds's claim that he was protected in his practice of polygamy by the provision for free exercise of religion contained in the First Amendment. This decision did not challenge the legitimacy of the Mormon church, but established that while the government has no business interfering in the beliefs of a religious group, it does have the right to intervene if the group's practices threaten important secular concerns. And monogamous marriage was felt to be a cornerstone of civilized society.[8]

The next two cases against the Mormons went much further. The practice of polygamy was used as the rationale for voiding the charter of the Mormon church and for declaring its property forfeit. The impact of those decisions forced the church to conform to social dictates, and in 1890 the church formally gave up the practice of plural marriage.

In this confrontation between the practices motivated by religious belief and the "sacred" institution of monogamous marriage, the court established its priorities between competing values. The social good, in this case, was deemed to outweigh in importance the personal freedoms guaranteed in the First Amendment.

The Mormon decision was pivotal in establishing an operational distinction between religious beliefs and actions, a distinction that has been maintained ever since. "Congress," the court states, "was deprived of all legislative power over mere opinion, but was left free to reach actions which were in violation of social duties or subversive of good order." [9]

The Supreme Court decision regarding the I-Am Movement raised very different questions about the relationship between religious freedom and social order. It addressed issues about the legitimacy of religious beliefs.

The I-Am Movement was founded by Guy W. Ballard, an engineer, who claimed to have been visited in 1930 by a divine messenger who revealed the Truth and bestowed upon him and his wife and son the gift of curing. By the mid-1930s, the movement had a following in the thousands and the Ballards were raking in money generated by sales of literature, records, and other material.

In 1944, the Ballards were convicted of using the mails to defraud. The indictments charged that the Ballards knew that their claims of supernatural visitation and their powers to heal were false and were made only to obtain money from those gullible enough to believe them. The Supreme Court's deliberation of this case resulted in a split decision. The majority opinion was that no agency of the state, including a jury, could decide about the validity of religious belief or experiences. "The religious views espoused by respondents might seem incredible, if not preposterous, to most people. But if those doctrines are subject to trial before a jury charged with finding their truth or falsity, then the same can be done with the religious beliefs of any sect. When the triers of fact undertake that task, they enter a forbidden domain. . . ." [10]

Justice Robert H. Jackson dissented from this opinion, arguing, "I do not see how we can separate an issue as to what is believed from consideration as to what is believeable." [11] The majority decision, he maintained, raised too many unanswerable questions: Who, for example, could challenge Guy Ballard's original experience (especially as he was dead)? Furthermore, though some people felt they had been duped by the Ballards, others claimed to have benefitted and been cured by them. Jackson believed that the determination of sincerity was beyond the powers of the courts. "I would dismiss the indictment and have done with this business of judicially examining other people's faiths." [12]

Over time, his opinion seems to have prevailed. Subsequent rulings have held that neither the truth nor the falsity of religious beliefs, nor the sincerity or lack of sincerity with which they are made, can become legal issues.[13]

These cases establish important precedents for evaluating the current cults and for determining what may or may not be done about them. The attempt of many cult critics to deny the religious legitimacy of these groups is futile. For it is not within the jurisdiction of the state to decide about the validity of the beliefs of an individual or a group. It is within the rights of the state, however, to determine whether the actions of groups violate the law or go against the public good. It is in this area that the courts can be effective in dealing with the abuses perpetrated by some of these groups. While some of the cases that have arisen concern relatively clear-cut issues—banking, currency, tax fraud, and foreign registration laws—others are far more ambiguous. When, for example, an ex-cult member sues a cult for psychological damage suffered while in the group, the court will have to decide which set of competing values are of paramount importance—the rights of the religious group or the rights of the individual. In fact, many of the cases brought against the cults are by parents who maintain that their children have been brainwashed or otherwise damaged by their cult involvement. These cases are even more philosophically tenuous, for three sets of rights must be assessed: those of the religious groups, those of the parents, and those of the children over whom the battle is being waged.

Legal quagmires are also created by the controversy over terms like *brainwashing* or *mental coercion* and the difficulties in establishing their empirical proof. These assertions are often complicated by the contradictory testimony of cult members, who maintain that their decision to be in a cult was freely made.

Future legal cases will undoubtedly address the issue of what constitutes free choice. Some lawyers believe that whatever cult members may assert, their rights have been intruded upon if they were solicited or indoctrinated without being told the identity of the group or about the nature of the life they would be expected to lead. Free choice, lawyers maintain, cannot be made without informed consent.[14] Bolstering this view are the rulings of two recent noncult cases. *Rogers* v. *Okin* established the right of confined mental patients to refuse treatment that would alter their personalities. The court established that one has a right to maintain one's own personality and also recognized the invalidity of taking a survey of patients after they had been treated and asking them whether they were better off than before. Another relevant case regarding informed consent is *Wyatt* v. *Stickney*, in which the court ruled that the Alabama prison that decided to use behavior modification as a way of treating prisoners could not do so without their prior consent. It maintained that behavior modification is no different from drug treatment and that the same kind of restrictions placed on mind-altering drugs ought to be placed on behavior-modification techniques. The legal recognition that these techniques are dangerous may, at some future point, bring about restrictions on the groups that now use them.

The real power of the law is to enforce some degree of conformity to the general moral code, so that behavior that is felt to be legally or morally wrong can be controlled. The courts have no other power. They cannot outlaw cults, nor should they. Not all cults are bad. Some have very beneficial effects. If the abuses of some are curbed, they may well serve a useful function.

The existence of cults, even the bad ones, is one of the costs of a democratic society. The freedoms they express by their very existence are not allowed in totalitarian states, and they must be protected. The essence of this dilemma is expressed in the following quotations:

> The Hare Krishna movement has begun making inroads into the Soviet Union. Their chanting and meditation appear to have found fertile ground in the Soviet Union, a country where the practice of yoga to achieve a higher level of consciousness has long had a following among intellectuals. Hare Krishna's publishing arm, Bhaktivedanta Book Trust of Los Angeles, was admitted to a 1979 Soviet book fair. By the fall of 1980, according to a Soviet industrial daily newspaper, the movement had spread as far as 2,000 miles east of Moscow to a Siberian City where a Hare Krishna chapter installed itself at the local House of Culture, under the guise of a health club. In the end, the law caught up with the chap-

ter leader, a young Russian named Yevgeny Tret-yakov. He was sentenced on an unspecified charge as a "social parasite" and the group, deprived of its spiritual leader, gradually fell apart.—*New York Times*, March 14, 1982.

The chief wrong which false prophets do to their following is not financial. . . . The real harm is on the mental and spiritual plane. There are those who hunger and thirst after high values which they feel wanting in their humdrum lives. They live in mental confusion or moral anarchy and seek vaguely for truth and beauty and moral support. When they are deluded and then disillusioned, cynicism and confusion follow. The wrong of these things, as I see it, is not in the money the victims part with half so much as in the mental and spiritual poison they get. But that is precisely the thing the Constitution put beyond the reach of the prosecutor, for the price of freedom of religion or of speech or of the press is that we must put up with, and even pay for, a good deal of rubbish.—Dissenting opinion of Justice Robert H. Jackson, I-Am Case, 1944.

Notes

Chapter 1: The Cult Phenomenon

1. William Wise, *Massacre at Mountain Meadows* (New York: Thomas Y. Crowell, 1976), p. 20.
2. Ibid., p. 40.
3. Marcia R. Rudin, "The Cult Phenomenon: Fad or Fact?" *New York University Review of Law and Social Change* 9, no. 1 (1979–1980): 18.
4. *Gallup Youth Survey* (New York: Associated Press, 1978, 1981).
5. Bella English, "The New Moonie Empire," *New York Daily News*, 5 May 1981.
6. Eugene H. Methvin, "Scientology: Anatomy of a Frightening Cult," *Reader's Digest*, May 1980, p. 89.
7. Carson Williams, "How Cults Bilk Us All," *Reader's Digest*, November 1979, p. 238.
8. Methvin, "Scientology," p. 89.
9. Flo Conway and Jim Siegelman, "Information Disease: Have Cults Created a New Mental Illness?" *Science Digest*, January 1982, p. 90.
10. Methvin, "Scientology," p. 88.

Chapter 2: Social Myths and Fairy Tales

1. Claude Lévi-Strauss, *Structural Anthropology* (Garden City, N.Y.: Doubleday, Anchor Books, 1967), p. 190.
2. Ibid., p. 196.

3. Norman Cohn, *The Pursuit of the Millennium* (New York: Harper & Row, Harper Torchbooks, 1961), p. 7.
4. Jeannie Mills, *Six Years with God: Life Inside Reverend Jim Jones's People's Temple* (New York: A & W, 1979), p. 122.
5. Bruno Bettelheim, *The Uses of Enchantment* (New York: Alfred A. Knopf, 1976), p. 40.
6. Ibid., p. 127.
7. Cohn, *Pursuit of the Millennium*, p. 8.
8. Bettelheim, *Uses of Enchantment*, p. 74.

Chapter 3: The Messiahs

1. "Messiah from the Midwest," *Time*, 4 December, 1978, p. 22.
2. Letter from L. Ron Hubbard to the Veterans Administration, October 15, 1947 (document seized from Scientology by the FBI and released under the Freedom of Information Act).
3. Claude Lévi-Strauss, *Structural Anthropology* (Garden City, N.Y.: Doubleday, Anchor Books, 1967), p. 169.

Chapter 4: Who Joins Cults

1. John G. Clark, Jr., "The Manipulation of Madness" (Paper presented in Hannover, West Germany, February 24, 1978), p. 12.
2. Jane Brody, "Personal Health" column, *New York Times*, 4 June 1980.
3. I. M. Lewis, *Ecstatic Religion: An Anthropological Study of Spirit Possession and Shamanism* (Middlesex, England: Penguin Books, 1971), p. 186.
4. John G. Clark, Jr., et al., "Destructive Cult Conversion: Theory, Research, and Treatment" (Boston: American Family Foundation, Center on Destructive Cultism, 1981), mimeographed, pp. 45–48.
5. Lawrence E. Hinkle, Jr., and Harold G. Wolff, "Communist Interrogation and Indoctrination of 'Enemies of the State,'" *Archives of Neurology and Psychiatry* 76, no. 2 (August 1956): pp. 161–164.

Chapter 5: The First Steps of Indoctrination

1. William Sargant, *Battle for the Mind: A Physiology of Conversion and Brainwashing* (Garden City, N.Y.: Doubleday, 1957), p. 170.
2. Christopher Edwards, *Crazy for God* (Englewood Cliffs, N.J.: Prentice-Hall, 1979), p. 133.
3. Private communication with Dr. John G. Clark, Jr.
4. Flo Conway and Jim Siegelman, *Snapping* (Philadelphia: J. B. Lippincott, 1978), p. 180.
5. Lawrence E. Hinkle, Jr., and Harold G. Wolff, "Communist Interrogation and Indoctrination of 'Enemies of the State,'" *Archives of Neurology and Psychiatry* 76, no. 2 (August 1956): 161–164.

Chapter 6: Breaking the Will

1. Charlotte Beradt, "The Third Reich of Dreams: How It Began," *The Third Reich of Dreams* (Chicago: Quadrangle Books, 1966).
2. Bruno Bettelheim, "An Essay" in Beradt, *Third Reich of Dreams*, p. 165.
3. Private communication with Dr. John G. Clark, Jr.
4. These dreams are briefly described by Bettelheim in Beradt, *Third Reich of Dreams*, pp. 156–157.
5. Private communication with ABC television producer Dan Goldfarb.
6. Bruno Bettelheim, *Surviving and Other Essays* (New York: Alfred A. Knopf, 1979), pp. 78–81.
7. Ibid., p. 116.
8. Ibid.
9. Gregory Bateson, *Steps to an Ecology of Mind* (San Francisco: Chandler, 1972), pp. 213–214.
10. Ibid., p. 214.

Chapter 7: The Physiology of Brainwashing

1. Steven Rose, *The Conscious Brain* (New York: Alfred A. Knopf, 1973), p. 176.

2. F. H. C. Crick, "Thinking About the Brain," *Scientific American* 241, no. 3 (September 1979): 226.

3. David H. Hubel, "The Brain," *Scientific American* 241, no. 3 (September 1979): 45, 46.

4. A. R. Luria, *The Mind of a Mnemonist* (Middlesex, England: Penguin Books, 1975), p. 10.

5. Duane P. Schultz, *Sensory Restriction: Effects on Behavior* (New York: Academic Press, 1965), pp. 6–7.

6. Jay T. Shurley, as quoted in Mark Kammerman, ed., *Sensory Isolation and Personality Change* (Springfield, Ill.: Charles C. Thomas, 1977), p. 263.

7. John C. Lilly, as quoted in Mark Kammerman, *Sensory Isolation*, p. 250.

8. Schultz, *Sensory Restriction*, p. 58.

9. Ibid., p. 62.

10. Shun-Ichi Saito, "Studies in Sensory Overload," *Tohoku Psychologica Folia* 30 (1971): 1–4.

11. Peter Suedfeld, as quoted in Kammerman, *Sensory Isolation*, p. 165.

12. Lilly, as quoted in Kammerman, *Sensory Isolation*, p. 251.

13. Seymour S. Kety, "Disorders of the Human Brain," *Scientific American* 241, no. 3 (September 1979): 213.

14. Ibid.

15. Ibid., p. 202.

16. Benjamin B. Wolman, ed., *Handbook of Dreams* (New York: Van Nostrand Reinhold, 1979), p. 26.

17. Private communication with Dr. John G. Clark, Jr.

18. Robert J. Lifton, *Thought Reform and Psychology of Totalism: A Study of "Brainwashing" in China* (New York: W. W. Norton), 1961.

Chapter 8: Getting Out

1. Ted Patrick, as quoted in Flo Conway and Jim Siegelman, *Snapping* (Philadelphia: J. B. Lippincott, 1978), p. 65.

2. Ibid., p. 66.

3. Ibid., p. 80.

4. Marc Galanter, "Psychological Induction into the Large-Group: Findings from a Contemporary Religious Sect" (Paper presented at the Annual Meeting of the American Psychiatric Association, Chicago), May 14, 1979.

5. Margaret Thaler Singer, "Coming Out of the Cults," *Psychology Today*, January 1979, p. 75.

6. Flo Conway and Jim Siegelman, "Information Disease: Have Cults Created a New Mental Illness?" *Science Digest*, January 1982, p. 92.

7. John G. Clark, Jr., et al., "Destructive Cult Conversion: Theory, Research, and Treatment" (Boston, American Family Foundation, Center on Destructive Cultism, 1981), mimeographed, pp. 58–59.

8. Singer, "Coming Out of the Cults," p. 76.

9. Ibid.

10. Conway and Siegelman, "Information Disease," pp. 88, 90.

11. Ibid.

12. Michael Langone, *The Advisor*, The American Family Foundation, Lexington, Mass., February–March 1982, vol. 4, no. 1, pp. 5–6.

13. Singer, "Coming Out of the Cults," p. 80.

14. Conway and Siegelman, "Information Disease," p. 92.

Chapter 9: Conclusion

1. See, for example, Marcia R. Rudin, "The Cult Phenomenon: Fad or Fact," *New York University Review of Law and Social Change* 9, no. 1 (1979–1980): 29–32; and Marcia R. Rudin and A. James Rudin, "New Religious Movements: Cults or Continuum" (Paper read at National Conference on Conversion, Coercion, and Commitment in New Religious Movements of the Graduate Theological Union, Berkeley, Calif., June 12, 1981), mimeographed, pp. 16–24.

2. The following articles have documented the stockpile of arms in some cults: Wayne King, "Krishna Arms Caches Draw Police Scrutiny in California," *New York Times*, 9 June 1980; Jo Thomas, "Some in Congress Seek Inquiries on Cult Activities,"

New York Times, 22 January 1979; Mark Forster, "Guru's Sect: Misgivings in Malibu," *Los Angeles Times*, 12 January 1979; "Two Ex-Aides Warn Guru Might Lead Sect to Violence," *Washington Post*, 26 November 1978.

3. "P. C. Operation Freakout," as it was called in Church of Scientology files, aimed at sending Paulette Cooper either to prison or to a mental hospital. See Gregory Gordon, "Scientologists Plotted to Frame a Critic as a Criminal, Files Show," *Boston Globe*, 24 November 1979; "Church of Scientology Implicated in Additional Plots, U.S. Asserts," *New York Times*, 4 December 1979; and Bruce Henderson, "Scientology Plot Against State Official," *Los Angeles Herald-Examiner*, 29 May 1980.

4. "Scientology Officials Arrested in Washington," Religious News Service Release, 16 August 1978, p. 23. See also Rudin and Rudin, "Cult Phenomenon," pp. 14–15.

5. David Berg's pamphlets as quoted in ADL Research Report, March 1979, pp. 2, 6. (ADL Research Report is a periodic report of the Anti-Defamation League of the B'nai B'rith, New York.)

6. Dennis King, *Our Town*, 10: 19 (2 September 1979), p. 8. U.S. Labor policy statement of April 21, 1978.

7. John Richard Burkholder, " 'The Law Knows No Heresy': Marginal Religious Movements and the Courts," in Irving I. Zaretsky and Mark P. Leone, eds., *Religious Movements in Contemporary America* (Princeton: Princeton University Press, 1974), p. 29.

8. Leo Pfeffer, "Legitimation of Marginal Religions," in Zaretsky and Leone, eds., *Religious Movements*, p. 16.

9. Burkholder, "Marginal Religious Movements," p. 30.

10. Opinion of Justice William O. Douglas in *United States* v. *Ballard* (1944), as quoted in Pfeffer, "Legitimation of Marginal Religions," p. 21.

11. Burkholder, "Marginal Religious Movements," p. 32.

12. Ibid., p. 33.

13. Ibid.

14. Private communication with attorney Herbert Rosedale.

Bibliography

Bateson, Gregory. *Steps to an Ecology of Mind.* San Francisco: Chandler, 1972.

Beradt, Charlotte. *The Third Reich of Dreams.* Chicago: Quadrangle Books, 1966. This little-known book provides an absolutely fascinating insight into how the Third Reich penetrated the psyches of Germans during those terrible years. In particular see Bruno Bettelheim's concluding essay.

Bettelheim, Bruno. *Surviving and Other Essays.* New York: Alfred A. Knopf, 1979.

Bettelheim, Bruno. *The Uses of Enchantment.* New York: Alfred A. Knopf, 1976.

Boettcher, Robert, with Freedman, Gordon L. *Gifts of Deceit.* New York: Holt, Rinehart and Winston, 1980.

Burkholder, John Richard. " 'The Law Knows No Heresy': Marginal Religious Movements and the Courts." In *Religious Movements in Contemporary America*, edited by Irving I. Zaretsky and Mark P. Leone. Princeton: Princeton University Press, 1974.

Clark, John G., Jr. "The Manipulation of Madness." Read in Hannover, West Germany, February 24, 1978. Mimeographed.

Clark, John G., Jr.; Langone, Michael D.; Daly, Roger C. B.; and Schecter, Robert E. "Destructive Cult Conversion: Theory, Research, and Treatment." Mimeographed. Boston: American Family Foundation, Center on Destructive Cultism, 1981.

Cohn, Norman. *The Pursuit of the Millennium.* New York: Harper & Row, Harper Torchbooks, 1961.

Conway, Flo, and Siegelman, Jim. "Information Disease: Have Cults Created a New Mental Illness?" *Science Digest*, January 1982, pp. 86–92.

Conway, Flo, and Siegelman, Jim. *Snapping*. Philadelphia: J. B. Lippincott, 1978.

Cooper, Paulette. *The Scandal of Scientology*. New York: Tower Publications, 1972.

Crick, F. H. C. "Thinking About the Brain." *Scientific American*, September 1979, pp. 219–232.

Edwards, Christopher. *Crazy for God*. Englewood Cliffs, N.J.: Prentice-Hall, 1979.

English, Bella. "The New Moonie Empire." *New York Daily News*, 4 May 1981.

Enroth, Ronald. *Youth, Brainwashing and the Extremist Cults*. Grand Rapids, Mich.: Zondervan, 1977.

Evans-Pritchard, E. E. *Witchcraft, Oracles and Magic Among the Azande*. Oxford, England: Clarendon Press, 1937.

Forster, Mark. "Guru's Sect: Misgivings in Malibu." *Los Angeles Times*, 12 January 1979.

Galanter, Marc. "Psychological Induction into the Large-Group: Findings from a Contemporary Religious Sect." Paper read at the American Psychological Association Annual Meeting, 14 May 1978, in Chicago. Mimeographed.

Galanter, Marc; Rabkin, Richard; Rabkin, Judith; and Deutsch, Alexander. "The 'Moonies': A Psychological Study of Conversion and Membership in a Contemporary Religious Sect." *American Journal of Psychiatry* 136 (1979): 165–169.

Gordon, Gregory. "Scientologists Plotted to Frame a Critic as a Criminal, Files Show." *Boston Globe*, 24 November 1979.

Harvey, Yoongsook Kim. *Six Korean Women: The Socialization of Shamans*. St. Paul, Minn.: West Publishing, 1979.

Henderson, Bruce. "Scientology Plot Against State Official." *Los Angeles Herald-Examiner*, 29 May 1980.

Hinkle, Lawrence E., Jr., and Wolff, Harold G. "Communist Interrogation and Indoctrination of 'Enemies of the State.' " *Archives of Neurology and Psychiatry* 76, no. 2 (1956): 115–174. This is perhaps the classic study of Communist brainwashing and interrogation techniques.

Hobsbawm, Eric. *Primitive Rebels: Studies in Archaic Forms of Social Movement in the 19th and 20th Centuries.* New York: Praeger, 1963.

Hubel, David H. "The Brain." *Scientific American,* September 1979, pp. 44–53.

Janeway, Elizabeth. *The Powers of the Weak.* New York: Alfred A. Knopf, 1980.

Kammerman, Mark, ed. *Sensory Isolation and Personality Change.* Springfield, Ill.: Charles C. Thomas, 1977.

Kaufman, Robert. *Inside Scientology: Or How I Found Scientology and Became Super Human.* New York: Olympia Press, 1972.

Kety, Seymour S. "Disorders of the Human Brain." *Scientific American,* September 1979, pp. 202–214.

King, Wayne. "Krishna Arms Caches Draws Police Scrutiny in California." *New York Times,* 9 June 1980.

Lévi-Strauss, Claude. *Structural Anthropology.* Garden City, N.Y.: Doubleday, Anchor Books, 1967. This collection contains a dense little essay called "The Effectiveness of Symbols," which describes shamanistic curing and compares it to psychiatric processes.

Lewis, I. M. *Ecstatic Religion: An Anthropological Study of Spirit Possession and Shamanism.* Middlesex, England: Penguin Books, 1971.

Lifton, Robert J. *The Life of the Self.* New York: Simon & Schuster, 1976.

Lifton, Robert J. *Thought Reform and Psychology of Totalism: A Study of "Brainwashing" in China.* New York: W. W. Norton, 1961.

Lilly, John C. "Mental Effects of Reduction of Ordinary Levels of Physical Stimuli on Intact, Healthy Persons." *Psychiatric Research Reports,* no. 5 (June 1956): p. 275.

Luria, A. R. *The Mind of a Mnemonist.* Middlesex, England: Penguin Books, 1975.

Mack, John E. *Nightmares and Human Conflict.* Boston: Little, Brown, 1970.

Methvin, Eugene H. "Scientology: Anatomy of a Frightening Cult." *Reader's Digest,* May 1980, pp. 86–91.

Mills, Jeannie. *Six Years with God: Life Inside Reverend Jim Jones's People's Temple.* New York: A & W, 1979.

Mitchell, Dave; Mitchell, Cathy; and Ofshe, Richard. *The Light on Synanon.* New York: Seaview Books, 1980.

Mooney, James. *The Ghost Dance Religion*. Chicago: University of Chicago Press, 1965.

Orwell, George. *The Collected Essays, Journalism and Letters of George Orwell*. Vol. 2, My Country Right or Left. Edited by Sonia Orwell and Ian Angus. New York: Harcourt, Brace & World, 1968.

Patrick, Ted, with Dulack, Tom. *Let Our Children Go*. New York: E. P. Dutton, Thomas Congdon Books, 1976.

Pfeffer, Leo. "Legitimation of Marginal Religions." *Religious Movements in Contemporary America*. Edited by Irving I. Zaretsky and Mark P. Leone. Princeton: Princeton University Press, 1974.

Rhinehart, Luke. *The Book of est*. New York: Holt, Rinehart and Winston, 1976.

Rudin, A. James, and Rudin, Marcia R. *Prison or Paradise*. Philadelphia: Fortress Press, 1980.

Rudin, Marcia R. "The Cult Phenomenon: Fad or Fact?" *New York University Review of Law and Social Change* 9, no. 1 (1979–1980): 17–32.

Rudin, Marcia R., and Rudin, A. James. "New Religious Movements: Cults or Continuum?" Paper read at National Conference on Conversion, Coercion, and Commitment in New Religious Movements, June 12, 1981, at the Graduate Theological Union, Berkeley, California. Mimeographed.

Saito, Shun-Ichi. "Studies in Sensory Overload." *Tohoku Psychologica Folia* 30 (1971): 1–4.

Sargant, William. *Battle for the Mind: A Physiology of Conversion and Brainwashing*. Garden City, N.Y.: Doubleday, 1957.

Schein, Edgar H. *Coercive Persuasion*. New York: W. W. Norton, 1961.

Schultz, Duane P. *Sensory Restriction: Effects on Behavior*. New York: Academic Press, 1965.

Shurley, Jay T. "Profound Experimental Sensory Isolation." *American Journal of Psychiatry* 117 (1960): pp. 254–267.

Simmonds, Robert B. "Conversion or Addiction." *American Behavioral Scientist* 20, no. 6 (1977): 909–924. Summarizes the available literature on the motivations for joining a Jesus movement.

Singer, Margaret Thaler. "Coming Out of the Cults." *Psychology Today*, January 1979, pp. 72–82.

Sontag, Frederick. *Sun Myung Moon and the Unification Church*.

Nashville: Abingdon, 1977. Sontag's book is virtually an authorized biography.

Sukhdeo, Hardat A. S. "A Clinician's Reflections on Some of the Problems of the Jewish Family in Contemporary America." Mimeographed.

Talman, Yonina. "Millenarism." *Encyclopedia of Social Sciences* 10 (1968): 349–362. For an overall view and summary of millenarian movements.

Tart, Charles T., ed. *Altered States of Consciousness.* New York: John Wiley & Sons, 1969.

Tetlock, Philip E., and Suedfeld, Peter. "Inducing Belief Instability Without a Persuasive Message: The Roles of Attitude Centrality, Individual Cognitive Differences, and Sensory Deprivation." *Canadian Journal of Behavioral Science* 8, no. 4 (1976): 324–333.

Thomas, Jo. "Some in Congress Seek Inquiries on Cult Activities." *New York Times*, 22 January 1979.

U.S., Congress, House Committee on Foreign Affairs Staff Investigative Group. *The Assassination of Representative Leo J. Ryan and the Jonestown Guyana Tragedy.* 96th Cong., 1st sess., 15 May 1979, pp. 1–777.

Williams, Carson. "How Cults Bilk Us All." *Reader's Digest*, November 1979, pp. 237–241.

Wise, William. *Massacre at Mountain Meadows.* New York: Thomas Y. Crowell, 1976.

Wolman, Benjamin B., ed. *Handbook of Dreams.* New York: Van Nostrand Reinhold, 1979.

Worsley, Peter. *The Trumpet Shall Sound.* New York: Schocken Books, 1968. For a detailed discussion of Cargo Cults throughout Melanesia.

Of General Interest

Father Divine is a fascinating character whose movement (the remains of it, at any rate) lives on in Conshohocken, Pennsylvania. For a lively, readable account of this "messiah," see:

Harris, Sara. *Father Divine, Holy Husband.* New York: Collier Books, 1953.

Interesting also are two articles written during Divine's heyday:

Moon, Henry Lee. "Thank You Father, So Sweet." *New Republic,* 16 September 1936, pp. 147–150.

McKelway, St. Clair, and Liebling, A. J. "Who Is This King of Glory?" *The New Yorker,* 13 June 1936, pp. 21–34; 20 June 1936, pp. 22–32; 27 June 1936, pp. 22–36.

For a comprehensive study of slavery in the American South that provides a larger context for Divine's and other black messianic movements, see:

Genovese, Eugene D. *Roll Jordan Roll.* New York: Pantheon Books, 1972.

There are any number of interesting books about Marcus Garvey and Garveyism, in particular:

Clarke, John Henry, ed. *Marcus Garvey and the Vision of Africa.* New York: Random House, 1974.

Cronon, Edmund David. *Black Moses.* Madison, Wisc.: University of Wisconsin Press, 1955.

Fax, Elton. *Garvey: The Story of a Pioneer Black Nationalist.* New York: Dodd, Mead, 1972.

There are a number of good books about Aimee Semple McPherson, including:

Thomas, Lately. *Storming Heaven.* New York: William Morrow, 1970.

I was most taken, however, with an essay by Carey McWilliams, which seems to capture Aimee's peculiar character:

McWilliams, Carey. "Sunlight in My Soul." In *The Aspirin Age,* edited by Isabel Leighton. New York: Simon & Schuster, 1949.

The Jonestown tapes, recorded by Jim Jones at Jonestown, Guyana, are available from the FBI under the Freedom of Information Act. These tapes constitute an extraordinary document. By the time Jones reached Guyana, he was no longer a charismatic leader; his ravings sound like those of someone halfway between an itinerant black preacher and a shopping-bag lady recently released from a state institution.

For good journalistic reports of the Jonestown tragedy, see:

"Nightmare in Jonestown." *Time*, 4 December 1978.

Axhelm, Peter; Lubenow, Gerald C.; Reese, Michael; Walters, Linda; Monroe, Vester. "The Cult of Death" and "The Emperor Jones." *Newsweek*, 4 December 1978.

Kilduff, Marshall, and Javers, Ron. *The Suicide Cult.* New York: Bantam Books, 1978.

There are many books describing the way the brain works. A straightforward though simplistic account is:

Hart, Leslie A. *How the Brain Works.* New York: Basic Books, 1975.

I relied most strongly on:

Rose, Steven. *The Conscious Brain.* New York: Alfred A. Knopf, 1973. Rose does not attempt to reduce an enormously complex subject to a few theories; furthermore, he presents the experimental evidence for all sides of a scientific controversy or question. Although his book is hard going for a layperson, his approach to the data inspires trust.

The entire September 1979 issue of *Scientific American* is devoted to the brain and is an invaluable source, although some of the material is beyond the comprehension of lay readers.

Index

DEMCO